Thoughts of an Ordinary Man

Ideas, Opinions and Stories that Reflect the Thoughts of an Ordinary Man. Probably Your Thoughts.

Jack Gorman

To order additional copies of this book, contact:
Xlibris Corporation
1-888-795-4274
www.Xlibris.com
Orders@Xlibris.com
58723

Thoughts
of
an
Ordinary
Man

Contents

Additional Rants Brought On By My Personal Distaste For A Biased And Reckless Media.

Forward

My desire, for quite a while, has been to write a book about my opinions of everything. Just MY OPINIONS. No references, no bibliographies, I am the only source.

When I rant and rave about politics, religion, or any other subjects which are normally considered taboo in polite company, it seems that most people tend to agree with me. Maybe they're just being polite, but that's a lot of polite people. News reports usually assure me that I'm wrong in my opinions but the many people I speak with on a daily basis seem to lean toward my beliefs, so I decided to compile my opinions into "Thoughts of an Ordinary Man" to see if ordinary people throughout the country tend to agree with me or if maybe I'm just nuts.

I'm led to believe that I'm an excessively pro-American, pro-religion, pro-everything conservative kind of guy but it seems to me that I am more mainstream. I love debating but rarely find too much disagreement with my humble opinions.

I am so pro-military that I find it hard not to choke up just reading about the dedication and sacrifices of our troops. Who doesn't?

I hate to think that America should change to accommodate new arrivals when I believe that they should adapt to our culture as immigrants have for four hundred years. My question is: if their desire is for America to change then why did they leave their homeland. I also believe that Italian food should taste like Italian food and not Mexican food just because jalapeños are all the rage at this time.

It drives me nuts how some first generation immigrants arrive here with a drive to succeed and great work ethics, and the third generation becomes typical, complacent citizens who add nothing more than another body in the work force, or worse, another drain on the economy.

I am very grateful to environmentalists for adding a conscience to our nation but why the heck do they always seem to become zealots who crush our ability to prosper?

I had found it interesting to study the differences between Shiites and Sunnis for years before the current war so I felt I was able to form opinions of my own which have proven true. My cause for confusion is why our leaders hadn't formed the same opinions. I don't feel like a Monday morning quarterback; I just feel that our leaders should have had the same opinions.

Like everyone else, I have opinions about Catholics, Protestants, Jews, Muslims, Blacks, Whites, Irish, Orientals, Democrats, Republicans, and the media and I don't think that my opinions will insult too many people because I think that these opinions are so close to the truth that they are shared by most honest people.

Like many, I am a casual reader of the Bible and the US Constitution and am still fascinated by both of these. I actually spend time thinking about whether I prefer the President of this great country to be a leader or a manager and I wonder why people who don't spend time on thoughts like these have a right to vote. I also question why a vote from a healthy, jobless, non tax paying, high school drop-out ne're-do-well cancels out the vote of a hard working, industrious, tax paying Samaritan.

If I were to read a book such as this for the first time, I would open to any chapter, any time I had a minute to spare. I have tried to write on subjects in such a way as to not expound on every avenue of every theme, but to give you fodder to ponder and compare my opinions to your own opinions.

I had recently received a birthday gift of a word game to be used on a Wii system. I believe it was a hint that I have been ignoring the video game system that has been impressing so many people, including my family. On the opening screen there is some quote from some ancient Greek regarding saying more with fewer words as opposed to saying less with more words. This struck a note with me in that the former appears to be my desire. I have wanted to reveal a thought in three to five minutes of reading; a thought which may bring you another fifteen minutes of contemplation. I don't seem to have a flair for easy flowing, flowery verbiage. Not being a gifted typist, and always being short of time, I have no choice but to say more with less. Although this may make for a slightly more intense read, the chapters are only a page long on average.

I have put a lifetime of personally formulated opinions in one book. To rationalize that this can't be all that I have experienced I will tell myself that the readers will place a million more hours to reconstitute these ideas back to their original values.

I have been casually writing these chapters as the thoughts occur to me. I've been jotting down notes, when a thought pops up, on pieces of scrap paper and in little note books, and then expounding on these note when I can get to a computer.

With no real sense of urgency to publish this book of ideas I've been watching one after another of these thoughts come to light on the news or as political platforms and decided to look into publishing so that it does not appear that my thoughts are simply reactions to, or regurgitations of, the thoughts of others. My goal is to publish only original thoughts.

Some one told me that each chapter should be a book of its own. I'm just too lazy to do the research to expound on each subject.

The books that I gravitate to are normally ones with shorter chapters so that I can read for a short time and still have a feeling of accomplishment. It's tough living life with such a short attention span. I'm sure that there's a name and a drug for this condition.

$1200

T alk about naiveté; it can strike anyone. Years ago as a young airman, I felt that I was in dire need of a car. As Viet Nam was just ending, a lot of guys were looking to get back to the real world and as the opportunities arose to go home one of my comrades was looking to sell his T'bird to get out from under the payments. The car was great. It was only a couple of years old, had a custom saloon back seat and was trimmed in crushed velvet and velour. It was quite the machine and I only needed twelve hundred bucks to own it.

The problem was, I had no established credit and the bank wanted a cosigner. I called my father and explained that I was planning on getting married and needed a car, and this was the one. I had a stable income and simply needed a cosigner. After already committing to my buddy, I was crushed when my father turned me down. I lost the car and for the next twenty years I had a certain resentment for his not helping me out when I needed him.

Years later, while reflecting back over life in general, it finally struck me as to what had really happened. My father was in no better position than I was to have a bank approve a loan. He had retired with a bad pension and was poor as a church mouse. As I thought back over my childhood I had never realized that we were poor. We seemed to have as much as anyone else had and maybe even more because my mother always knew how to get the kids off the New York City streets without spending very much money.

I don't think my old man ever made more than five hundred bucks a month in his whole life. By not telling me the truth, he let me hold a twenty year grudge. He may even have assumed that I knew our family's financial situation.

He had been a garbage man for the City of New York and in the 1960's he had made a bad decision. He was at his twenty one year mark and was eligible for retirement when a major strike occurred. On the table were the retirement conditions. Afraid that he may be required to stay thirty years or maybe till age fifty five, he elected to retire immediately. Most of his buddies were a year behind him and didn't have the option to retire.

It turned out to be one of his worst decisions. The workers won the strike and ended up with a great pay raise and maintained their retirement benefits.

My father ended up with his five hundred bucks, and his buddies who retired the following year had great pensions and bought nice homes. My father struggled just to stay in the basement apartment.

Even if I was oblivious, he must have known we were poor.

A simple explanation would have resulted in, at worst, ten minutes of discomfort for both of us and ten more minutes of disappointment, instead of twenty years of hard feelings.

33% Bob

I'll tell you about a crazy character I had met. This guy was retired Army and was looking to spend some money in the worst way. His wife had decided that they should have an Acura but their credit rating said that they should be driving a Yugo.

Bob took an Acura for a test drive and was a little erratic with his driving prowess. I told him that he drove like a one legged drunk and he assured me that he was sober. He did however, have a prosthesis. He had about the best attitude I had ever seen under that circumstance.

It seems that after retiring from the Army he took a job training tractor trailer drivers. One of the new drivers had slipped the clutch while backing up and 'gloved' Bob's leg. Gloving means to slip the flesh off a leg as a glove would be removed from a hand. The gloving required the removal of half of his leg to facilitate the prosthesis. Bob came complete with 8 by 10's of the before and after the operation in full color.

He explained the unfortunate part of living in Virginia at the time even though he was a native New Yorker.

New York is the town where one can spill a cup of coffee and be awarded six million dollars by a jury. His situation was radically different. He informed me that in Virginia, on the job injuries were limited by worker's comp to one hundred thousand dollars.

His one hundred thousand went: thirty three to his attorney, thirty three to his wife, and thirty three to Bob. His wife had decided that his thirty three thousand would purchase the new car.

A short while after the purchase, a change occurred in Bob's life. He told me that he was awakened one morning with a loud thump which woke him up then knocked him back out. He said that his wife had beat him on the head with his wooden leg while he was sleeping and then ran away with his leg so he couldn't chase her.

According to him, she had cleaned out the remainder of his savings, taken her money, and ran off to Puerto Rico with her new boyfriend; leaving their teenage son with Bob.

Bob was now left with his portion of a twelve hundred dollar a month Army pension which was being split with her, one leg, a two hundred fifty pound, unemployed teenage son to feed, and no job prospects.

I ran into Bob from time to time and he would keep me abreast of his current situations. After procuring a new leg he found a job driving a handicap transport mini-bus. I haven't got a clue how he managed this with his right leg missing and not being able to help carry the handicapped passengers in and out of the bus.

After a short while he drove the mini-bus into the side of a truck and once again found himself among the unemployed. Virginia had another unique rule which affected Bob. A retired GI is ineligible for unemployment for five quarters because he has technically quit his job. I was always curious why the attorney who took the thirty three thousand dollars for a worker's comp case which Bob probably would have won with no assistance at all, didn't provide follow up advice out of common decency.

He eventually ended up moving from one friend's apartment to another and somehow, even lost his Acura.

He said that he had learned a lesson that he had already suspected, don't piss off a Puerto Rican woman.

911 And What to Do?

It's a strange feeling to watch a national emergency unfold and not have a planned response. On 9/11/2001 as the country watched the first attack and then the second and then the third, each serviceman knew what to do; where to report to to prepare to perform his duties. Each fireman and cop knew where to go. All disaster preparedness personnel had a recall preparation to adhere to. Even Guard and Reservists had a game-plan to follow.

For civilians, the event was extraordinarily scary. Not knowing what was to come next and having no idea what to do or where to go can be terrifying because of a feeling of helplessness. What should you do? What about your family? Few civilians ever make contingency plans for emergencies because you're not taught to.

Most Americans under forty years old have never seen a discernible threat to the American population and so, have never had to even think about what to do if the situation arose.

Perhaps that is one of the reasons that so many men and women enlisted shortly afterwards. Not just for patriotic reasons, but also to become a part of the group that does not feel helpless and confused in emergencies. People want to be part of a team; and part of the team that is in control when it counts. There's a comfort in being in the know, having a duty to perform, and having a planned response.

For the first time in my adult life, I was an outsider. I also stood by and waited for someone else to respond. With no duties to perform to help protect America, I was dependent on someone else to do their duty. It's not a secure feeling to be one of the masses; to have no way to help and no idea of what to do next. Thank God for the ones who do.

2000 Year Old Church

I'm asked from time to time why I still go to church. I'm given a hundred reasons why I shouldn't. There are many valid reasons why one may question the justification for organized religion in today's world.

Each day it seems like there is a new accusation of child molestation, sexual abuse, larceny, bilking the congregation, and whatever else can be imagined when humans are involved in positions of religious authority. I can personally cite quite a few instances.

I remember meeting someone who needed a car pretty badly but had credit so torn up that no bank wanted to take a risk on him for less than 20% interest plus a huge down payment. He bought a used Camry and promised to use it to restructure his credit. A couple of years later I saw him again. This time he was driving a new Cadillac, trimmed in gold, and sporting some very expensive whitewalls.

I asked him how he had turned everything around so well and the answer was," God !".

The truth was that he had managed to buy some time on a local AM religious radio station and had set up a pretty sweet deal for himself and his wife. He was building a decent following of faithful listeners who were starting to make some substantial donations to his new 'over the airwaves' church. One elderly believer had recently donated a $38,000 piece of real estate.

Another preacher I had met had asked to lease a new car for him and his wife. We developed a great rapport and I joked with him about being one of the few preachers that I had encountered that wasn't a bandit[1]. With not too much work I was able to qualify them with a good bank. We shook hands and I told him that I was going to have to change my opinion of preachers. Less than a year later he returned and asked how to get his name off the contract and put it solely on his wife. When I explained that it was a very difficult request, I asked why? He said that he was about to kick his wife's butt to the curb and wanted her stuck with the car. Good thing that I hadn't really changed my opinion about preachers.

Many Catholics believe that the clergy had become largely homosexual, and that lifestyle violates the belief of a large portion of the congregation. It may be that the Church has become a comfortable vocation for homosexual males and that homosexual priests provide a role model which attracts more homosexuals. Unfortunately, some of these priests became sexual predators and many lives were ruined, casting a distasteful cloud over the Church.

With these and so many other problems with clergy, I can see why so many people have lost their faith in organized religion.

My answer as to why I still attend Mass is: the Church is 2000 years old. When Jesus handed the reigns to Peter He set a standard which will continue till the end of the world. There have been many bumps in the road throughout the twenty decades such as an occasional bad Pope, an English king who kicked the Church to the curb for his personal convenience, and a number of opportunists who have lost the true path.

I'm sure that none of this has come as a surprise to God, and I consider these as a few bumps in a long, long road. Long after we are gone the Church will continue and will cycle up and down in popularity. My job today is to ensure that there are at least some people who will speak well of the true Church.

---

[1]   A term used in retail for customers with bad credit or underhanded in their business dealings.

5030

The following was response to an article presented on a website dedicated to the ex-residents of my old neighborhood in uptown Manhattan. The article contained old newspaper accounts of an explosion in a telephone company building, on my block, which killed about twenty workers, mostly women, and injured about a hundred more in the early 1960's. It happened while I was home for lunch from grade school and I was probably the first one on the scene. For the near future, the block resembled later pictures form Beirut or Baghdad.

The address of the building was 5030 Broadway.

Hearing glass shattering while home for lunch from GSS, I ran to the street to see the results of the catastrophe. At 8 years old the first thing noticeable was broken glass everywhere. Injured women were hanging from the phone company windows trying to escape the building. No adults were any where to be seen so I ran back to my apartment to have my mother call the police.

It was difficult to comprehend what had actually happened, even as I was able to watch everything unfold.

Throughout the rest of the day and night it was more confusion than anything else. The major questions seemed to be accounting for who might be missing.

My grandmother owned a luncheonette on Broadway, not 50 yards from the phone company building, and so, knew many of the girls who worked at 5030 and ate lunch at the store. The anticipation as the names were released was the worst.

The men of the block reacted by running into the building, as you would hope a man would react when challenged, and the women were on the spot providing aid and comfort to the injured. In retrospect, it makes you proud to have come from those people, in that time.

With all the carnage, in retrospect, it did not seem to have very much negative effect for the kids on the block. As time went on it simply became part of our way of life.

I don't remember any psychologists providing counseling and I don't remember any lingering mental problems with the kids. Everyone just adapted.

As the cleanup began and the reconstruction went on forever, it was quite an interesting block to live on. The construction equipment and rubble piles became quite the playground. Being that young, we were more likely to make the situation as positive as possible. Without anyone explaining how mentally incapacitated we should have become – we didn't.

I wonder how that would have compared to a similar event today.

A Layman's Look at the Banking Crisis

The government is asking for about $4,000.00 from each American family. Who gets this money that is coming from my family's budget and why are the details so complicated that ordinary people can't understand the situation?

How many of my family's dollars will go to the managers and speculators, as bonuses? These maggots have been profiting far beyond the comprehension of ordinary people. If I start a business and fail due to mismanagement or if I simply mismanage my family, I don't expect to be rewarded by someone else.

Where the heck did this $700 billion figure come from? It sounds like more money than the US has transacted from Jamestown till 1960 cumulative. It's an ungodly amount of money. An amount so large that most people simply blow it off because it can't be real. $700 billion seems like enough money to pay five years of mortgage for every homeowner in default.

And, this should go to a government controlled agency to bail out known losers? Based on the proven history of other government controlled agencies it will be tripled, and we all know that.

I wouldn't give a dime! Wall Street's bad performers would simply fail – and be prosecuted publicly. Assets would be seized, including their protected Florida mansions which were purchased as insurance against their criminal actions. Accounts, assets, vehicles, and yachts of these perpetrators would all be confiscated and liquidated. The CEOs would have no more assets than the janitor who has lost his job due to the mismanagement of the CEO.

People who purchased real estate far beyond their means, because they were misled by unscrupulous realtors and lenders, would be offered assistance through new mortgages for extended terms guaranteed by the confiscated assets of the criminals. These longer mortgages would offer homeowners an opportunity to maintain their homes and not become a burden on everyone else.

Only *victims* would be assisted. I would love to see this put to a vote before my family's money is commited.

Any excess money from the funds confiscated from these crooks should be deposited into my 401K account to replace what was stolen by these scum.

Alabama 1950

I heard a discussion on Iraqi insurgents which answered the question I had been pondering. The subject is often clouded with talk of al-queda and other outsiders who are interfering in the Iraq problem. Those enemies can be handled. The reason the Sunni insurgents are so difficult to defeat is 'Alabama 1950'.

What I mean by this is: imagine an outside power such as Germany, if we had lost WWII, or Russia, if we had lost the Cold War, coming into Alabama in 1950 and setting down a new set of rules. What if the Whites in Alabama were told that the Blacks were now in charge and their new rulings would be enforced through the power of the new conquerors. After generations of White rule, it ends overnight. How hard do you think those white Alabama boys would fight against Blacks and the invaders? There would be a hell of a resistance.

How compassionate do you believe the Blacks would be toward the Whites as the roles were reversed and where would the White anger be directed as their homes, businesses, and farms were confiscated?

In Iraq we were the invaders. The Sunni minority had been in control over the majority Shiites for many years. Power was stripped immediately from the Sunnis and given to the Shiites. The Shiites were not prepared, nor trained to receive the power and therefore complicated the transition even further.

Picture the resistance that the Alabama boys would have offered and apply it to Iraq today. As the atrocities began to mount against the Sunnis a lot of scores were being settled on both sides.

Although the transition may have been handled differently, there is very little variation that could have been expected for the outcome.

Both sides have to adjust and some memories will never die. Think of the controversy over the Confederate flag in the Southern states a century and a half after our Civil War.

I do believe that the problems with outsiders such as al-queda or Iran may someday ease up but old memories die hard.

Altar Girls

One to the changes to the Catholic Church has been the introduction of altar girls. With less and less interest in the Church today it must be difficult to attract altar boys.

When I was a kid, many of the boys became altar boys or choir boys. It seemed kind of a natural thing to do prior to high school. It didn't insinuate a propensity toward a religious vocation; it was just the thing to do. Some of the parents who were directly off the boat hoped that their sons would become priests because the mother of a priest was held in high regard back in the old country and she could receive special privileges for donating a son to the priesthood or a daughter to the convent.

Each gender had a distinct path. Girls were not altar boys. Boys were altar boys.

It does seem a bit unusual to see girls on the altar serving in a position that was exclusively reserved for boys. The Church has been making quite a few adaptations in order to survive extinction.

Some say that the Church should stand fast and if only a small number of the faithful remain then that small group of the truly faithful will rekindle the Church in the future. They believe that if the Church continues the metamorphosis, the Church will no longer have a basis from which to return.

Others say that whatever it takes to survive as a Church today is okay. Questions about gender, homosexuality, fidelity, and abortion are all on the table when it comes to surviving. It's a tough call.

I, personally, feel that the problems of the Catholic Church today are just a blip on the radar screen. With a two thousand year history of surviving, directly back to the pact between Jesus and Saint Peter, today's problems will pass. Every other Christian church was an offshoot of the Catholic Church. Corrupt Popes and immoral priests who had damaged the Church from time to time have come and gone and will continue to come and go as long as human beings are associated with the Church. Through all the trials and tribulations of twenty centuries, the Catholic Church still survives. This might very well be the time when it all crashes down, but I doubt it, as long as the core stays strong.

Ambulance Drivers

Hearing the stories of bravery and integrity of modern emergency responders it puts them on a plateau above the norm. Although underpaid, it has made these professions very desirable for young men and women.

Many kids aspire to become EMT's (the new name for ambulance drivers). It seems that the EMT's are better trained than ever and have more life saving equipment than even hospitals used to have.

The EMT training courses are tough and it gets progressively harder and harder to advance in the career field while staying current on the new life saving equipment that becomes available each day. In an emergency you'd probably prefer to have an EMT on the scene than anyone beside an ER doc.

This is a far cry from the days when it seemed that the ambulance was there simply to get you to the hospital.

In conversation today with EMT's the talk is usually about great stories of blood and guts where lives were saved through the quick actions of the techs. There is a great pride in saving lives and a job well done.

The first ambulance story I can remember was from a New York City ambulance driver from the days when NYC was notorious for corruption. The story was about the skill level of the ambulance drivers when responding to DOA's.

The most skilled could enter an apartment and immediately size up the situation. Through years of experience and OJT it was immediately apparent where the deceased hid their money and valuables. Some people were the 'under the mattress' type; some were the 'mayonnaise jar' in the refrigerator type.

The very best 'first responders' were able to discern this quickly enough to pocket the booty before the police arrived and the goods had to be split with them. From the stories I remember, there was a great pride in a job well done – and done quickly.

American Steel

If you want to know what makes America great, start your list and I'll give you a great one – American steel. Very few countries can make steel like the US. Maybe Germany, maybe Japan, but not many more. Drop a Leatherman knife in a bucket of water and take it out ten years later and I'll bet it still looks like new. Nothing holds an edge like it.

The competitors have started manufacturing in China and they are NOT the same. They are just cheaper. They have the same old reliable names but they are junk. A person who makes a living with his tools, owns a Leatherman. It may cost more but it lasts forever.

One of the reasons that the Japanese have been able to impact the auto industry is the overall quality of the metal. The Koreans are nowhere near the quality although they may get there soon.

As we share our technology, we do tend to get our asses kicked. The Japanese have begun to crush us in more than just electronics. The mastery of steel manufacturing has made them world class. It must be some battle for them to keep the Koreans a step behind.

I had once watched a Dent Doctor plying his trade at an Acura dealership. After pushing dents out of a number of Japanese cars, he came upon a Korean made Ford and when he attempted to push the dent out, his tool pushed right through the sheet metal and the car had to be sent to the body shop for major body repair. His profits were shot for the day and I'm sure that he never again confused a Korean made car for a Japanese made car.

The next question is: with all the advanced tech companies, such as Boeing, dealing with China, how long will it be till we lose our edge in the world of steel to China. We may then have access to good quality steel but we won't be able to afford it, even at the reduced price, because we'll all be unemployed.

Another DMV Story

With all the complaints I have about DMV, I had heard a great story which I still remember well. A few years ago the Virginia DMV was making some changes to save money. The plan was to close on Wednesdays and to also close some of the DMV offices around the state[2].

As this was happening I had an opportunity to speak with someone directly involved. She told me of the happenings at her particular site.

It appears that a DMV official was dispatched from Richmond to speak with the workers at the affected offices.

Upon arriving, he called the girls together for the announcements. First, he said, DMV offices will be closing on Wednesdays in an effort to save money. Second; after next Tuesday you will no longer need to come to work because this office has been scheduled to close permanently.

As the story went; the girls huddled up for a minute and advised the DMV official of a modification. They told the gentleman that there would be a slight change to the plan; they did not feel well enough to continue to work and needed to go home sick. He could service the customers till they closed the following week.

If you're going out – go out in style!

---

[2] It seems to me that DMVs and ABCs are the two money generators in most states. Everything else, such as roads, schools, etc., consumes money. Why would you cut back on income generators?

Antidisestablishmentarianism

Funny what we can remember and when we can remember it. In grade school, my mother was considerate enough to procure a tutor for me to help me overcome my desire to fail. It was quite embarrassing for me at the time to have the teenage girl from down the block interfere with my playtime and, of course everyone on the block knew that I had a tutor.

Beside the benefit she provided to me of saving me from losing a year of my educational life by being left back, she taught me how to spell antidisestablishmentarianism.

Presented to me as the longest word in the dictionary, it seemed challenging enough to tackle. Today, every one of my kids can spell it and so can my siblings. I don't even think there are many dictionaries left that even list the word but, if the occasion arises, I can handle it.

This could be similar in nature as to why kids seem to excel at language studies and anything else that they, themselves, decide is worth learning.

Oh yeah, it's a noun, meaning a political philosophy opposed to the separation of church and state.

Arab Tricks

I learned a lesson in real estate and cultural relations while selling my house. A full price offer came from a buyer who introduced himself to me as an Egyptian Christian. This was supposed to add credibility to his offer. I answered enough of his friendly questions to reveal that I had purchased another home and would be closing shortly. He appeared friendly enough and even brought his family to see the house as they made their move-in plans.

The scam you ask?

As my realtor placed all other offers on the back burner and put the sale pending sign up, the zinger came. After I committed to the new house and potentially lost my 'hot' buyers, he proposed a new offer that was thousands lower than his first written offer. One thing that he learned about real estate law is that offers are not binding. The combination of cultural low ethics and utilization of real estate loopholes is becoming a more common practice according to some realtors.

The goal is to make an attractive offer to ensure that you commit to your next house while losing your hot buyers. This often works because most Americans have a different ethics standard than some of these maggots have.

Needless to say, I dismissed this worm and kept my house on the market. As the next culturally similar maggot attempted the same ploy I accepted his offer and requested a twenty five thousand dollar, non-refundable deposit up front. That was a portion of real estate law that he was not so schooled in and he vanished to find another honest American to scam.

Luckily, I found an honest buyer who purchased my house at a fair price. As home sales are becoming more critical today, I wonder if these ethically challenged maggots are becoming more common?

So as not to appear bigoted by a single mid east cultural experience, let me share some more mid east cultural stories.

While still living in the aforementioned house, the 9/11 tragedy occurred. A day of two later, while leaving my house to take my daughter to school, the black Suburbans sped into the cul-de-sac opposite my front door. As they stopped, the flack vested, crew-cutted agents swarmed over one of the houses. It was the first one of these operations that I had seen in real life and I didn't have a clue as to what was going on.

A few days later, after I had a chance to read the paper and do a bit of inquiring, I bumped into my neighbor who reflected on how terrible Said had been treated. Looking for agreement from me on the mistreatment, he was looking to the wrong person.

I explained my opinion of the situation: first, his name is Said, second, he has a mobile basketball backboard in his driveway but no kids; and he, obviously, has never used it, third, he owns a cigar store in a strip mall but I have never seen a customer in his store and he manages to afford a home in a very nice area, fourth, his house happens to be the only house in the whole development that borders on the airport runway, and lastly, the search of his house revealed ten passports which have been used for travel to Lebanon.

Unfortunately, you never seem to find out the rest of the story in these cases. Guess I should have been a cop.

Here's another true story. Years ago I worked as a recruiter in the North East and covered many of the colleges and universities. Some times I would have some time to kill and would have the opportunity to speak with some of the students in a non-professional setting. My favorite was to speak with Palestinian students at schools such as Fairleigh Dickenson University in New Jersey.

I would start off a conversation with a young Palestinian by inquiring as to his opinion of the mid east situation. The initial response was always the same, "it is unfortunate that peace cannot exist in the mid east."

Next, I would agree the peace should prevail because the Jews and the Palestinians were brothers who shared a common ancestry if you go back far enough. I could always see the jaw tightening a bit at this point. I always believed that these engineering students were a potential threat.

Next I would ask why the Palestinians had never taken it upon themselves to accomplish what the Jews had accomplished with Israel and asked whether the Jews should have a stake in Israel after developing the land when no one else had accomplished such a marvelous feat.

As the blood vessels bulged in the forehead I knew that the brotherhood, living in peace line was a crock. It didn't take much to have a Palestinian reveal his true ambition of death to all Jews. I could have had them screaming that out loud if I had had the desire.

I was always amazed at the training that we were providing to these kids that positioned them to inflict damage in the future. I guess the driving force was the money brought to the universities by these kids. The engineering schools were overwhelmingly foreigners because the American kids were studying sociology and psychology. Without foreign kids in the programs the engineering schools would have collapsed. I wonder if the foreign students in the flying programs prior to 9/11 were what kept those programs afloat.

Are There Enough of Us

This is a question I posed prior to the 2008 Presidential election. Although not a dyed in the wool McCain supporter, I did believe that he was owed a debt for his sacrifices and that he more closely represented traditional American values.

The opposition appeared to resent these values which they believed to be represented by older White Christians, and in particular, George Bush. This ended up eliminating McCain and even Hillary.

Traditional American values, from family to religion, were becoming demonized and obsolete. Believing that these values had made America strong and free, I was concerned that this freedom was neither appreciated nor understood and would be used to eliminate its very foundation in an attempt to obtain personal gain, instigated by empty promises.

According to the pollsters virtually *every* Black in America will be voting for Obama. This is understandable to me because of the 'loyalty factor'.

My concern is that virtually every Muslim, every radical, everyone wanting a free handout, every terrorist sympathizer, every liberal university professor, every illegal alien who has managed to get a vote, every homeless person who is carried to the polls for a free meal, everyone who desires America to subordinate itself to UN domination, every college student who wants to be a hippy when they grow up, and everyone who values Oprah and Hollywood over traditional family values, will be voting for Obama.

To these people character is meaningless. They possess a blind faith in their new messiah which cannot be swayed by truth.

Are there enough traditional people who will show up to vote?

You've gotta touch everyone you know because they are touching their people!

Ban Guns

I sometimes wish that guns, as well as many other questionable items, had never been invented; but they had. Our Constitution gives our citizens the right to bear arms as per the Second Amendment.

As a homeowner with a family I appreciate the playing field being balanced in the event some 'crazy' attempts to harm my family. Being armed allows me to provide the proper protection for my family and possessions until proper authorities can respond with assistance. It also permits me to contain a situation so that a police officer will not have to sacrifice his life in order to protect mine after a break-in. Break-ins occur all the time so I am not so naïve as to think that I am immune.

Being properly armed and trained I am not as worried about protecting my family and home as I am about the efforts of some people to confiscate my weapons and tilt the field in favor of the criminal who will always have access to weapons. Living as a sheep, at the mercy of the odds that the next break-in will be at someone else's home instead of mine is not as comfortable as I like to be.

Why these people are so hell bent on taking my protection away absolutely befuddles me. These are normally the same people who desire lighter sentences for the criminals who would murder an innocent family.

As usual, I have a recommendation. I propose that those who want guns removed from the homes of law abiding citizens make a positive gesture to show their good intent and investment in their beliefs. Place signs on their lawns and windows saying, "*There are no guns on these premises*".

In a society shaped by those more liberal than I, I would like to see a firm commitment from them to confirm their belief that all people are basically good.

I, personally, would like a perpetrator to at least think twice before entering my home. He should have to be willing to risk his life to do so because, Lord knows, there is very little deterrence in the legal system.

Banking Crisis Hiding the Energy Crisis

With all the attention given to the banking crisis right now, what's going on with the oil crisis? How much profit will be scammed by the oil producers while the limelight is on the banks?

I have an opinion on the energy situation. The first candidate to recommend my opinion gets my vote.

If the energy crisis is real and there is a real desire to solve it, it will proceed like this: NASA will redirect 75% of its efforts toward alternative energy solutions. 25% will remain supporting the current space obligations.

NASA has funding, America's best scientists and physicists, facilities, and a non-profit mission directed by the US government. Command and support structures are already in place and need to be redirected to handle the proclaimed energy crisis which is proving to be a threat to our national security.

If one solution is the development of better batteries for gas-free vehicles then why haven't we redirected our resources already?

How serious are we to solve this problem? It appears to me that the solution, so far, has been to raise the price of gas and oil to the breaking point and then to lower it slightly till the heat dissipates. It's worked well enough so far to have us paying twice what we were paying just a few years ago and feeling happy that it's no longer above $4.00.

A drastic reduction of oil needs will disempower our enemies and make us the world leaders again.

Until such a move is made I have to assume that the only ones concerned about oil prices and availability are the consumers.

BBC

For years I have enjoyed listening to BBC2 radio. I like it for the radio personalities and especially for the music, which caters to people my age. The personalities which appear during the morning and early afternoon (eastern US time) are great. The added benefit of listening to a British radio station is that, occasionally, American personalities are interviewed.

With the interviewees feeling safe by 3000 miles of ocean, it is interesting to hear these interviews. When the American public exploded over the Dixie Chicks' unfavorable comments about George Bush I was not very surprised because I had become used to this type of diatribe.

While appearing on foreign radio it has become a symbol of status to demean the US.

Bonnie Raitt's interview on the Steve Wright show was a classic. Her denigration of the US government made me assume that she would never consider returning to such a hell on earth.

The boys of Crosby, Still, and Nash have a ball knocking the US. The British audience must have a very dour picture of us when American stars are so vocal about their distain for our lifestyle.

Randy Newman had a blast knocking the Bush Administration. He announced to a British audience that it was not the worst in history as long as you can compare it to Hitler or ancient Rome.

Antonio Banderas presented a documentary about the glory of Che Guevara. Che is hyped as a hero throughout the anti-imperialist audience. His romantic presentation of Che and Castro shows his true feelings. He didn't emmigrate to Cuba to make his fortune though.

The British have leaned left for quite a while now and some American stars feel that they can make brownie points with the enlightened British audience by tossing their loyalties aside. Maybe these are their true feelings and they feel more comfortable with a civilized audience rather than the American barbarians. They always seem to come home though. Britain (once called Great Britain) does not have enough of an attraction to keep them there. Maybe it's the image of a nation of men with crooked teeth who seem to wish that they were girls. Maybe it's because these stars eventually realize that many of the talented British had emmigrated to the US because of the opportunities here and the demanding taxes there. Maybe, because there is no place in the world that can match the US; especially when there are so few places that would allow a citizen to publicly debase their own country while on another country's national radio station and then allow them to return home to make more money for the next trip abroad.

With the advent of world wide radio access through a home computer, more Americans can stay in touch with their favorite stars as they travel the world as our roving ambassadors. Perhaps, it won't be just the Dixie Chicks who get to share their adventures abroad with their fans back home who support them so lavishly with their capitalist dollars. The socialist dollars don't spend so well.

Benefit of the Sellout

When the glass is half full, it's just that much more that's gonna spill when you knock it over! (Jack 33:2)

With jobs moving overseas and mills closing throughout the northern rustbelt, there has got to be an upside. To the unemployed New Yorkers, Ohioans, Michiganers, and Pennsylvanians, it may be hard to believe this.

As we sell out to China, Mexico, and any other place that can help to destroy the American infrastructure to benefit the companies that can best take advantage of foreign slave labor for increased profit, the hope is that it will eventually reach a breaking point.

Many American workers are already at the breaking point because they cannot feed their families, they can, however, buy imported goods at a lower cost from Wal-Mart.

When the breaking point is reached nationally, and we can no longer afford to import because we have made them richer than we are (case in point is Japan who was in the 'China slot' in the 60's and now uses us for cheap labor) there will be an opportunity for us to build new factories and mills which will be needed to provide America with goods which we will no longer be able to afford to import. These new factories and mills will be more efficient to operate and the increased cost effectiveness may once again provide gainful employment to permit America to cycle back to the power position.

Although most of the great nations of the past were never able to recover, we may be the exception.

Bennigans Closing

The evening news just announced that a restaurant chain known as Bennigans has closed all locations without advanced notice. They mentioned that the owners have filed for chapter 11 protection from creditors. The portion of the report that concerned me most was the interview with the worker who showed up for work only to find the doors locked and no paycheck waiting for him.

The owners will probably be protected enough by the chapter 11 to re-emerge as another restaurant and retain their management positions with little disruption of their lives.

My concern is for the workers who had their trust betrayed and will now lose their apartments, cars, and maybe even their furniture for non-payment. Although I am far from being tagged as a Liberal, I do believe that an owner has an intrinsic responsibility to those who he has agreed to take on as an employee, provided the employee was a responsible asset.

I don't agree that protection tools such as chapter 11s, 7s, and 13s were designed to protect only the managers and owners; especially when these people may drive a bus over their employees to protect themselves.

The average restaurant employee will make less than thirty five thousand dollars. The affect of no pay for a few weeks till another job is found or until unemployment kicks in is catastrophic.

Although the six figure person may be affected, the worst case situation is for them to end up in an apartment temporarily as opposed to the apartment dwelling worker who can end up on the street.

It seems that from Bennigans to Wall Street the story is the same.

Bigotry

I was sometimes a bit uncomfortable around them. We're supposed to all be the same but there are enough differences, in my mind, to justify hanging with my own kind. The language may be the same but the jargon is definitely not what I'm comfortable with. When they talk, it takes some adjustment to be 100% sure what they are saying.

They dress different too. I kind of prefer my look but I have to admit the some of their accessories look sharp.

The hair styles are different and I notice lately that some of my own kind are starting to get haircuts like theirs. That does tend to irritate them a bit and they call us wannabes. They think that they are the real deal because they're cool right now.

Deep down they really wish that they were more like us. We are better educated and have a higher class life style. Their life is more physical; ours is generally more intellectual. Not that one is better than the other but it is a bit different and birds of a feather . . .

They are not all the same anyway. Some are worse than others, especially when that macho stuff flairs up. They fight with themselves as much as with anyone else.

It's not that they're better or worse than us, just different enough to make each feel a bit more comfortable with our own kind.

When their kids hang out with my kids they seem to get along great. The schools are a great place for kids to spend eight hours together and learn how to get along so the next generation will coexist much better.

I have had some job experiences where I worked side by side with a number of them and after a while we got along great. At lunch time though, we did go our separate ways. Some of that crap that they call food is not what I prefer to eat so I would tend to drift back to what I am more comfortable with.

It was always a unique learning experience though to spend a bit of time with them occasionally and not have all my opinions of them formed by the evening news.

I am sure that we are all equal when you get past the stereotyping but I was still Air Force and they were still soldiers.

What were you thinking?

Black Moms

The strongest segment of America today has got to be single Black mothers. Many times left on their own with a child (or children), they are left to provide for themselves. With the wage scale so low for so many, they have become ingenious at surviving and providing a home for their children.

Whatever the societal reasons, the results are the same; it is often up to a single mom to compete in an environment that is set up to require two bread winners with good paying jobs.

So many of these moms manage to put a roof over their heads, food on the table, clothes on their backs, a vehicle to drive, and somehow, even some occasional entertainment. This is often done with jobs that are slightly above minimum wage. Most other families couldn't make it with three times that income.

Their brilliance shows through their networking abilities to share child care, work additional jobs under the table, and procure food and clothing at better pricing than their 'well to do' counterparts could ever do.

So many obstacles are placed in their way each day that it becomes more and more amazing how they adapt. As gas and heating costs rise, percentage wise, it is even more catastrophic to their budget.

With little possibility to establish strong credit the 'buy here, pay here' car and furniture dealers often prey like vultures on these 'need buyers' offering inferior quality goods with no warranties. Still, these women overcome!

Living in a community where so many others survive under the same conditions, it may seem typical to struggle so hard. Happening as often as it does today, it may seem normal to be abandoned by the father of the child, so expectations are low, stigmas are reduced, and 'handling the situation' begins without so much social pressure.

If the men in the community knew and appreciated the magic of these women they wouldn't be walking away at such a terrible rate. In spite of the extraordinary efforts of these men to obliterate their society through the destruction of the family unit, the power of these women is ensuring their survivability.

Black Wednesday

J ust want to mention a coincidence which is interesting to me. I had always been accusatory of George Soros, a Hungarian born Democrat who is a major contributor to the left cause. His mission had been to defeat Bush and he is a major contributor to organizations such as moveon.org.

I have also been accusing him, as well as the left wing media of purposely undermining public confidence in the American economy to 'crush' our economy so that they might offer a messiah with the theme of 'CHANGE' to offer hope to the voting masses and to the world.

Here's one more bit of verifiable information. George Soros is famous (or infamous) for 'breaking the Bank of England' on Black Wednesday 9/16/1992.

As England resisted falling in line with the European currencies, Soros speculated against the pound and made a fortune while destroying retirement funds for many of British. To me, this sounds very familiar to our situation today. 16 years later his skill is perfected.

I have always claimed that he will not be satisfied until we are subordinate to the UN.

As England resisted the European Union he taught them a lesson.

Look it up. I did!

Body By Chance?

G et a cut; watch it heal. Walk in a room and see one picture frame out of ten slightly crooked. Feel a baby's forehead and tell if there's a fever. Smell smoke from a fire. Smell lasagna cooking. Hear a steak sizzling. Hear a voice and instantly identify age, gender, nationality, and region. Convert ½ pound of food into eight hours of manual labor. Identify and appreciate a Picasso. Fly a 150 ton airplane. Build a 150 ton airplane. Write a computer program for facial recognition. Grow two cells into a breathing baby in nine months.

All this, and a million more features, in a human being. And you believe there's no God!

Bush Skunks Arabs?

Just a thought from an ordinary man about the economy. I remember reading about the dealings of Donald Trump. In my humble interpretation it appears that the 'Don' had sold New York properties to Japan a number of years ago, went bankrupt, crushed the market, then bought back a good bit at a bargain rate thereby cementing his fortune. This may or may not have happened that way but it sure sounds good to me and I hope that it happened exactly that way; America needs a hero from time to time.

Along the same line, I have been watching a couple of trillion dollars change hands within the US to help put the economy straight. Then I read that the Arabs have just taken more than a two trillion dollar loss due to investments gone bad and oil prices, and in my romantic mind I'm wondering about the correlation between this and my interpretation of the Trump story.

If this, by any chance, were to be true wouldn't Bush be remembered in a much better light than he is presently?

Buy a Car for Half Price

I'm always amazed at the clever ways that are presented to deceive the consumer. Although I am cautious of government regulation of virtually anything, predatory preying on unsuspecting consumers through blatant deceit may be one of the exceptions even I could approve of.

Dishonest and misleading advertising has become the norm with so many retailers that it's sometimes almost impossible to discern the truth in any type of ad. It also makes it difficult for an honest business to compete because the truth rarely looks as attractive as a well fabricated lie. The retailer's attorneys will argue that their ad is never, technically, a lie. Somewhere in the presentation there is a disclaimer which reveals the deception to a buyer who is adequately schooled in bullshit detection. Unfortunately, most buyers are not.

An ad should be able to be read one time by an average citizen of average intelligence and be completely understood. Asterisks and reduced size print have no place in an honest ad.

An example of what I consider to be a dishonest ad is presented by a local car dealership. The ad says, "why pay $18,000 for this vehicle elsewhere when you can buy the same car here for $10,000".

Even armed with the knowledge of the scam, I found it impossible to find the disclaimer. Using a 50 inch plasma TV and a DVR to slow down and pause the commercial I still couldn't identify the scam. Upon further review, the disclaimer was to be found on their website if you had enough site-surfing savvy to find that small print. Apparently, that still rides the legal edge which keeps it legit. Not moral nor ethical, but legit.

The actual scam is: you are not buying the $10,000 vehicle as you would expect. You are buying three years of the vehicle for the ten grand and owe an additional ten grand or so at the end of the three years if you want to own it. The tax is additional and must be paid against the whole value of vehicle, in that particular state, even though you are buying less than half of the car. This, obviously, is a lease and therefore the additional leasing fees must also be paid.

To the average consumer, who may purchase 6-10 new cars in a lifetime, this is a scam, a lie told in such a way as to make one believe that the vehicle can be bought for almost half price simply by choosing one dealership over another. The consumer believes that if it appears on a legitimate TV station, that the commercial must pass muster and should be safe to believe; WRONG!

Although the customer should have the right to assume this.

Besides the customer who is being robbed, the other victim is the dealership who strives to deal fairly. Not only did they lose the opportunity to present a legitimate offer to the customer; but the customer often attributes the bad experience to the brand and not to the dealership leaving the buyer gun shy of the brand. The customer may also believe at that point that that car is truly only worth $10,000.

I believe that if the stipulations required to obtain a particular deal are so detailed and complicated that they can't fit in a 30 second commercial then buy a 60 second commercial; or better yet, reduce the stipulations and present an honest offer to the buyer.

In the electronics world, prices are advertised reflecting a rebate which you must pay upfront and pray that it is honored sometime in the future – if you can jump through all the hoops required to claim the rebate and then can remember, six weeks later, to try to reach a live party if the rebate check hadn't arrived. This is another shameful practice based on deceit, in my opinion. Advertised prices should truthfully tell you what you should expect to write your check for before taxes.

A retail industry so embedded in deception can never police itself. Honest vendors can rarely compete in such an arena. That is why I believe that only a higher authority can force the necessary changes.

The naive will say that an honest business will always win in the end. The pragmatic will say, "Bull". If someone promises an average consumer a product for half price, believe me, they will have his attention and he won't be looking for the seller with the higher price.

The saying goes, "buyer beware". Too bad

Can Civilians Hire Hit Men to Handle Terrorist Problems?

With the continuous beheadings of innocent civilians in the Islamic world it begs the question: what are the legal implications if donations are collected to thwart terrorists?

Upon viewing the staging of beheadings and watching the gut wrenching interviews with widows of civilian workers killed while attempting to rebuild Iraq it is obvious that these terrorists are unconventionally cruel and inhuman. They are not acting in a rational or civilized manner and are causing ungodly pain to the victims and the victim's families. The victims are not military personnel. They are civilians who are rebuilding Iraq to better the lives of the population.

To eliminate the desire of these terrorists to continue these sick habits and to provide incentives to their peers and superiors to dissuade these maggots, unorthodox methods must be taken. These methods may seem alien to Americans, but they are well understood by the perpetrators.

I propose that donations be solicited to hire contractors to apply Islamic-like pressure to these terrorists to make their actions less desirable. Islamic-like pressure would be defined as the identification of these terrorists, and the destruction of all they deem precious, such as homes, superiors, and everything that their superiors hold valuable. *Their history should be eliminated as well as their opportunity to enter paradise intact.* Internal pressure from surviving friends, peers, and superiors concerned about the safety of themselves, their families, and possessions may be what is required to provide the incentive to help solve this problem.

Current, civilized prevention methods are ineffective, weak and foolish in the eyes of these radicals. A bounty paid to contractors who know the methods, and are prepared to apply them would be money well spent and will give donors the satisfaction of knowing that they really made a difference in the elimination of potential terrorist recruits.

My original question is: what are the legal ramifications for U.S. civilians who donate and arrange contracts for this purpose?

I wrote this after watching the beheadings of Americans and knowing of the atrocities perpetrated on innocent civilians in Iraq. It was frustrating to believe that our only response is so politically correct that it poses no incentive for the killing to end.

Our leaders can't seem to comprehend that our responses are considered a sign of weakness by our enemies. This failure to understand the enemy and retaliate accordingly has resulted in an unfair loss of military and civilian lives.

Can Real People Make an Impact?

C an real people make an impact on the government or even the community? Not a chance! Real people work for a living and today, real people work more than eight hours each day. Spare time is spent with family or accomplishing the necessary tasks to live a normal life such as mowing the lawn or paying bills or, God forbid, having a hobby.

So, who does that leave to make an impact? Who can run for office in the community or in the government? Normal people can't even make time for the PTA.

Retirees can make the time. That does lean the candidates toward the right though. Remember about young people having no heart if not liberal and old people having no brain if not conservative . . . Not so many retirees today have the kind of money it takes to enter the political arena. Time without money can be useless in politics.

The wealthy can enter the political arena. The wealthy are also better positioned to draw on the support of wealthy supporters because the non-wealthy normally do not frequent the same country club.

Many politicians are very well to do. If not rich when entering politics, then surely rich as favors are repaid for the support given. That seems to me to be a tough society to enter. A real person does not normally get positioned to participate in those circles.

Women can sometimes afford to enter politics if supported by a successful husband who can keep the family afloat if her political career crashes and burns. This is similar to why there are so many successful women in the real estate business. Few men can afford six months without a salary to try to establish a career, as is the requirement to enter the real estate world.

Although most buyers may traditionally feel more comfortable transacting large purchases with a man, (for archaic and prejudicial reasons) men are less likely to have a financially supportive spouse who could enable them to enter the real estate field to be positioned to take advantage of this. This is why men who can manage to break into real estate have so much better chance to succeed. Where women are so much more adept at the finer points of showing a home, traditional buyers often prefer to deal with men when it comes to spending their money.

It seems fairly common to see many of the successful female politicians having husbands who are successful in business. Note, I will have to research whether these husbands become even more successful when the wives are positioned to grant favors back to their business.

Another group that is noteworthy is the professional politician. The person who lives a life preparing to be a politician.

I believe that Bill Clinton was a classic case of this. Coming from a small town with meager financial assets, he became the most powerful man in the world. Along the path it seems like he built a great network to foster his career. I remember watching reports of 'friends of Bill'. Captains of industry, Hollywood moguls, and other very impressive people in his personal circle who would meet with Bill and Hillary somewhere in Northern California, I believe, to hash out plans of attack for Bill's challenges.

Strangely enough, it seems that there were a number of power players who came from his home town and rocketed to the zenith of their fields.

That was one strong network and I wonder how many reciprocating favors occurred beyond the obvious prison pardons at the end of his career.

How else though could a man of humble beginnings compete in the political arena?

Out of the categories that make up the bulk of the politicians: the retired, the rich, women, the connivers, which were envisioned by the founding fathers?

It seems like they pictured citizen politicians who would serve for a short period and then return to their normal lives. Politics was not to be their normal lives and politicians were not to serve forever. Washington elected not to serve a third term so as not to be confused with royalty. The royalty in America today are the Kennedy's and the Bush's. The women I had described are Boxer, Polosi, and Hillary. The connivers are John Kerry and John Edwards. Would any of these be acceptable to our founding fathers?

Which are normal citizens who were drafted from the populace to serve and then return? None! I, personally, would prefer a representative who did not want the job. If it's a job you want – I don't want you!

Canon

A number of years ago it was announced that Canon was coming to Virginia. Incentives were made, which probably included some tax breaks, but the potential benefits to Newport News, Virginia were to be massive. Tons of jobs and benefits to Virginians were promised. A new partnership between Virginia and Japan was promised and there was to be prosperity.

A beautiful facility was built in Newport News and the grounds were immaculate. Lots of local laborers were employed. The truth of the matter however, is that the majority of the workers in the plant are hired through temp agencies meaning that they do not share in the promised prosperity. They do not receive the promised benefits. No medical, no dental, no retirement, no profit sharing, and no job security. Local temp agencies provide, what is termed, cattle calls for local laborers to see who will get to work on the Canon assembly line at a reduced wage, but with the hopes that they may qualify for one of the prized 'permanent' positions. The permanent positions provide good benefits but a modest salary. In my opinion, this is to provide a dependency on the company.

Progression in the company is generally limited for non-Japanese. Upper management positions are filled by young Japanese executives who periodically arrive from Japan. I have met a number of them and they are impressive. They speak a fair bit of English and are very enthusiastic. They appear similar to young military officers at a new overseas duty station and their tour of duty is about the same length. When it was said that, what Japan could not do militarily, they would accomplish economically, it was the truth.

When Canon first arrived, the speculation was that local suppliers would benefit from contracts to supply the needed supplies for the plant. What actually happened was that Canon brought their own suppliers for belts, moldings, glass, etc. and these suppliers also utilize many temp workers.

The recent announcements in Virginia are of Canon's plans to expand in the area again and even the governor has a word of thanks for the benevolent Japanese. The promise is for a $600 million investment in another facility and 1000 jobs. My question is: how many will be permanent jobs for Virginians? If 800 of these jobs are to be temp positions, it simply means that there will be 800 more hopefuls who will grow older with no benefits and no security established for their futures. 800 more laborers that will become dependent on the government in the future.

Charlie's Factory

Let me tell you about a real life situation regarding the threat of outsourcing American jobs. Speaking with a very good friend of mine who is as reliable a source as anyone can be, I learned of a real world situation that exists throughout the whole country.

Deep in the heart of Tennessee sits a factory that manufactures labels for clothing. The factory has provided work for a number of Tennessee families for quite a few years. Under the present ownership, the atmosphere in the work area has deteriorated to the extent that my friend, who was a senior employee, had been asked to address certain problems to the owner. Believing that the gripes were legitimate he presented them to the owner. The owner's response was enough to have my friend elect to separate from his job.

The owner said that rather than make the requested changes, he would prefer to outsource future work to China. Offers were already being made to him that were much more lucrative and he would enjoy greater profits, with no personnel problems, by simply becoming the distributor of the product that he would allow to be manufactured by the Chinese.

I'm not sure if that qualifies as extortion or if it is just a case of a greedy bastard with no morals putting the screws to hard working Americans simply because he can.

I would tend to believe that the people who make these decisions are not normally the ones who had built the business. I would picture that it was the second or third generation who took no pride in the business and who simply enjoyed the fruits of their predecessor's work.

Upon discussing this with others, I hear of similar cases that are happening all over America. Another case is with a company which procures large rolls of paper and cuts and processes the paper into products for distribution. The owner can maximize his profits by having the rolls shipped to China for processing and simply distribute the finished product to his present customers. With virtual slave labor, the shipping around the world, twice, still turns a greater profit, and by kicking his workers to the curb he no longer would have to contend with health benefits, pensions, social security, or any other costs that are required for a labor force.

I wonder, in these cases, if the customer knows of the circumstances. And would it make a difference to the customer. With the acceptance of Wal-Mart in our lives the answer is probably no.

I seem to remember that when Sam Walton was alive, the Wal-Mart commercials boasted 'proudly made in America'. Today you would be hard pressed to find a single item in Wal-Mart that is made in America. This one company alone has probably put a million Americans out of work to take advantage of the benefits of slave labor. Did Sam ever know of the metamorphosis?

The sell out is made every day by millions and millions of American consumers who patronize Wal-Mart for lower prices. It has reached a position where virtually all of Wal-Mart's competitors have emulated the process of dumping American made products for Chinese knockoffs. Walk the aisles of Target or Kmart and try to find a single item made in the USA.

A number of years ago while in Australia, I was told that imported vehicles were subject to a tariff of up to 100%. The purpose was to keep Australians working. The problem, however, was that few people wanted Australian cars because of the poor quality.

To protect a domestic industry such as automobiles, or steam irons, or children's shoes, there must be safeguards to protect the American consumers from the greedy bastards that would take advantage of protectionism to provide a less than perfect product.

I would recommend that an American automobile protected from competition by government tariffs should subject itself to guarantees of product quality which could be ensured by real warrantees equal to or greater than the imports. I would also expect accountability down to the worker on the assembly line whose career was salvaged through tariffs.

Accountability must also be exempt from union interference so that the actual culture becomes one where only perfection is tolerated. To salvage an industry, sacrifices must be made by all involved.

The current rationalization is that Americans must retrain for the new economy. This is simply a line of crap to attempt to justify the screwing of the American worker to maximize profits through the utilization of slave labor rather than paying a fair wage to an American worker.

It seems that simply buying products made in America would be a solution but we are far beyond that. Most consumers have no access to products that are made domestically. Home Depot, Lowes, and most other chains have virtually eliminated products made in America.

I was surprised as I watched Home Depot stock decline as all indicators show a gold mine. Could it be that a corporation that would allow the decimation of American jobs could possibly be a little underhanded in their business practices and profit reporting?

Chick Filet Cell Phone Story

I can still remember one of my first encounters with 'the cell phone'. While at lunch with a good friend at a Chick Filet we watched a mother and daughter at a neighboring table. As we both have daughters, we were commenting to each other as to how nice it was to see a mother and daughter spending time together and having such great conversation. The mom looked very pleased to be spending such quality time together.

This all ended rather abruptly with the ringing of the daughter's cell phone. As mom sat there completely ignored, the daughter proceeded to spend the rest of the lunch time making small talk on the phone.

The conversation included everything from Oprah Winfrey to Saturday night's plans. Mom was completely excluded from the conversation. My opinion of the cell phone was established at that moment.

Yes, mom should have taken control of the situation, but she didn't; and a thousand times since then I have seen similar situations where cell phone etiquette is lacking.

Today, texting has added a double whammy. My texting acronym for my daughter to use when she receives a text message is WMD (with my dad). Our time together is not to be interrupted.

Chris Dodd

I just heard a sickening interview between Don Imus and Chris Dodd of Connecticut. The same Dodd who has been taking money and favors from the perpetrators of the money crisis as he sat in his decision making capacity as a US senator. The same low integrity Dodd who threw Lieberman under a bus when he thought it was politically expedient and then tried to kiss his ass when the people of Connecticut elected him anyway.

He did a 10 minute blood fest of how he has slept only four hours a night for seven days to try to save us from Bush and McCain; the same McCain who was his close friend on previous interviews prior to the campaign. He spewed every Democrat talking point I had already heard numerous times this morning on the talk shows. If he has been spending every minute trying to save the country when the hell did he have the time to rehearse and coordinate the political talking points?

He proved that the 'best defense is an offence'. A few days ago I was hoping that he would be looking at a prison sentence for unscrupulous money lending activities and today he is successfully reassigning blame and building points for a Democratic win.

How does Dodd, the chairman of the Senate Banking, Housing and Urban Affairs Committee, avoid a prison sentence and then publicly lie his butt off on the facts.

This clown now has a major say in the decision to pay out $700 billion. His cohorts now have a second chance to avoid prosecution for their activities and maybe even enrichen themselves further. Where the hell is the FBI?

Dodd claims that the basis of the whole problem is the mortgage situation which $700 billion may fix. I say, if that is so, take the $700 billion of our money off the table and force the lenders to offer 50 or 60 year mortgages, at stable rates, to the home owners in 'equity only' or 'ARMs'. At best, it will allow home owners to stay in their homes without 'our' money, and at least, it will hold off the 'dumping' of these homes and allow them to be spread out for years to protect property values.

Let the criminals who profited by setting up the ARMs and duping the ignorant, absorb the hit. ALL their assets should be confiscated and compiled to fund this activity. Again – where the hell is the FBI?

I wrote this shortly after hearing that there would be a $700 billion bailout of Wall Street and the banking industry.

Cigarettes

I've always had mixed feelings on cigarettes. Do I hate them or despise them?

I'm not a believer in excessive government control over the private practices of adults – HOWEVER COMMA!

Smoking in one's home or alone in a private vehicle sure seems to be within the rights of a citizen. If, however, the smoking leads to excessive medical bills, I don't want to pay them for the underinsured smoker. I also would not expect someone else to pay my bills if I drive without a seatbelt or ride a motorcycle without a helmet.

Watching a minivan full of kids with an adult smoking does make me think about the rights of minors to breathe clean air.

Sometimes it goes beyond kids. If your boss lights up in your office or at a luncheon should your career be jeopardized by your objecting or should there be protection provided to you through prohibition?

At a meal, the most disgusting sight is to see a cigarette butt ground out in mashed potatoes. It shows a definite lack of class!

Restaurants do provide nonsmoking sections but the persons closest to that section always seems to enjoy the benefit of cigarette smoke without even having to light up. While smokers seem to build up a tolerance to the sordid aroma, nonsmokers do not. It will kill the flavor of a $50.00 steak. Smokers, having diminished taste buds, may not worry about this but everyone else does.

Because the pressure has been so high on smokers lately there is a natural defensiveness built up among smokers regarding their right to smoke. I don't want to take away their right to smoke but I don't want them to continue to take away my right not to smoke. The correlation would be: if my addiction was to the aroma of mace I wouldn't expect a non-macer to put up with my spraying of mace near their meals, in public transportation, or anywhere that it may offend them. I would also expect that far more people have died from cigarettes than from mace.

Another bothersome result of cigarette smoking is the loss of production time in the workplace. My personal observation has been as follows: a smoke break can require the worker to secure their equipment, grab their coats and cigarettes, leave the work area to go to the outside smoking area, light up and smoke one or two cigarettes, return to the work area, and bring their equipment back into production. Although it may seem like a five minute break, it is normally 15 to 20 minutes multiplied by 3 to 4 times per day. If this is in doubt, have your smokers punch out whenever their production halts for a smoke break. That extra hour or so per day is often times absorbed by the nonsmokers who are covering their tasks and taking their messages while they are out of the area.

Debts Owed

The American Civil War cost 618,000 lives. 360,000 Northern soldiers and 258,000 Confederate soldiers. This was a massive number of American losses; more than any war before or after. To put it in perspective, Iraq and Afghanistan have cost us about 4,000 lives. Viet Nam had cost us about 58,000 American lives. The Battle of Gettysburg alone cost over 23,000 lives from each side. The numbers were massive.

The war was fought to stop the secession of the Southern States from the United States. One of the reasons for the South's desire to secede was the fear that Northern pressure would eventually end slavery and cause turmoil due to their primarily agricultural economy. They perceived that slave labor was the key to their economic survival.

The Northern Army was comprised of soldiers who had no obvious benefit from a salvaged Union. They were often recent immigrants, Blacks, and poor laborers to whom the 'cause' was obscure. Where most Southern soldiers believed in their 'cause', which was the survival of their lifestyle; often, the only known motivator for Northern soldiers was the freeing of the Southern slaves. Abolitionists and books such as 'Uncle Tom's Cabin' had made Northerners aware of the slave situation in the South.

To the 360,000 Northern soldiers who died in the freeing of the slaves, a debt is owed. To the 416,000 American soldiers who died to free Europe and Asia during World War II, a debt is owed. To the 36,000 American soldiers who died to keep South Korea free from communism, a debt is owed.

Who acknowledges the debt? Do the South Koreans who are now some of the most prosperous people on earth appreciate the American sacrifice? They can see the North Korean alternative lifestyle where poverty, famine, and tyranny rule and still their youth are not appreciative.

Do the Europeans who are now two and three generations removed from WWII have any gratitude toward America for the terrible sacrifices that were made to free their families to flourish in freedom so that free Europeans can enjoy their prosperity today?

Does American Black youth appreciate the lives that were lost to provide their pathway to freedom? Thousands of Americans gave all. Northern Black soldiers as well as most other Union soldiers already had their freedom. They had no need to fight for a 'cause', such as the Confederates did, believing that their security and freedom were at stake. It was a true sacrifice to go to war to end slavery.

In spite of the obstacles that can still face Blacks today, do people take time to give thanks to the memory of those who gave the ultimate sacrifice for a stranger's freedom?

In a culture where most Americans believe that they are owed everything, it is unusual to feel a debt to anyone.

I am extremely grateful that my family risked everything to make it to America so that I might have the opportunities that I have enjoyed. If they could view my life, I hope that they would be glad that they made the decisions that they had made. Do my kids ever think about how different their lives would be if not for the sacrifices of others? Do yours?

Cops Eat Free

I just got a call from someone saying that they are collecting for the 'fallen policemen's family fund'. I told him that I want my number and name removed immediately from his call list.

For a number of years my wife had donated to these maggots and others with similar sounding names fearing that if she did not, that there would be repercussions.

I had personally spoken with these people before and asked directly, "what percentage of my donation do you keep?". The answer is 85%. For those who are math challenged that means that only $.15 goes to the 'fallen policemen's' family. You would have to donate $400 just to get them a tank of gas!

I grew up in New York City where other types of donations were made to cops at that time.

I had tried to charge a cop for a sandwich when I started working in a deli as a kid, and the boss went nuts. He said that cops eat for free or there won't be a cop there when you need one. Lots of cops ate lots of food there but we were never robbed. I hope that he was wrong about the reason for the free food but the belief at that time was that cops were corrupt and vindictive. These thoughts stay with you forever.

Growing up in that atmosphere fostered my wife's belief that, if you don't donate to the policemen of firemen's fund, your name goes on a 'list'. I believe that the donation solicitors who keep 85% of the donation know about, and exploit this fear.

If law enforcement knew that their name was being used to extort these donations, of which the overwhelming majority went to the solicitor, would they break the relationship and find a more efficient and trustworthy method to support their needs?

If there was a way to actually donate 100% to the direct needs of a family of a fallen public servant I'd be in and would be giving directly instead of through the United Way as I do now.

Even if the percentages were reversed and 15% went to administrative fees, I'd be in; but not for the crooked, extortion smelling program that exists now. The word track that is used by the telemarketers fosters my belief. It is very clever and I wish that I had had an opportunity to record it.

If you receive such a call, ask about the percentage kept by the solicitors and donate wisely.

Demands on My Time

Family, friends, career, all make demands on my time. Some of these demands I don't mind; some I do. As long as my life is still defined by the Earth's correlation to a burning ball of hydrogen, I still only get 24 hours to use per day. With such limitations, I do prize each available hour and I prefer to be the one who decides how they're spent.

Certain time demands are inevitable, expected, and accepted but some of the latest ones are definitely not appreciated.

I expect time wasted for commuting, shopping, gassing of vehicles, paying bills, and numerous other necessary activities but there are new additions every day which are demanding way too much of my time.

Each quarter, or so, I receive my life insurance package of probably 25 pages. Whatever language it may be in, it sure doesn't seem like English. I always assumed that that was why I pay so much money to my agent.

I am asked to review this to ensure that I am properly insured. To possibly understand this, as a layman, requires reference to the glossary in that back of the booklet and comparisons to my previous year's booklet to compare any changes which are normally my responsibility to catch and contest.

This is compounded by the requested yearly review with my agent who would like to sell me additional insurance. When my car insurance paperwork arrives, it's the same story. I can't imagine how much time I must devote to this each review period.

Each time I purchase any electronic or entertainment item I am expected to read a poorly written handbook before operating the item. I have to learn how to program, set timers, reprogram remotes, study warranty requirements and limitations, and whatever else they consider important. Then I get to attempt to retrieve my rebate which, God forbid, could have been simply reduced from the selling price at the store.

To buy a new computer I get to learn a new windows program all over again and reload all the necessary programs so that I can find out which are obsolete and must be updated or repurchased.

When buying a new car, I not only have to read numerous manuals to learn the new safety and convenience features but I have to struggle through setting the clock, which is never set the same way the last clock was set. The radio is even a greater travesty. The manufacturer expects me to figure out which radio I have, out of the myriad of possibilities, and then, which magic combination of buttons performs the desired secret maneuver. I will never get to enjoy all the special features I had paid for without first investing an evening or two to the manual. Synching the phone to the radio to comply with state law while driving is the latest requirement.

Where does this time possibly come from? There is a finite number of hours in one's life.

Upgrade any program on your computer, or make a purchase, and you find the disclaimer which can be pages long. You've seen it; you have to click either 'I agree' or 'I disagree'. Of course most people simply click 'I agree" to get to the program. What was said in that disclaimer that could be detrimental to you? No one knows because it is written so long and tedious that no one has ever read one.

Apply for a credit card and see how much reading is required to protect yourself. The print is so small and complicated that it is virtually never read. Most people do not know that the listed interest rate is only at the discretion of the credit card company. The rate can be changed if deemed necessary by the grantor. How many people would still sign if they knew this? Burying it deep in the disclaimer section on the back of the application keeps it from becoming apparent. Few people have the time to do such extensive reading just to get another credit card. Making such huge demands on our time and allowing us to bypass the reading of these extensive documents, although jeopardizing our rights, is the normal path of least resistance. These demands on our time are an unwelcome invasion into our lives. To make it worse, it appears to be increasing proportionately to the decrease in our available free time.

Desert Boots Ended My Empire

As a kid in New York City I thought that I had found my true career path. My mother let me borrow my father's shoe shine box, while he was at work, and unbeknownst to him, so that I could earn enough to buy one of my own. My father would have killed me if he had known. His shoe shine box was stored in his locked closet which no one had access to but him; or so he thought. My mother always had access to everything in the apartment. Nothing stopped my mother from her missions.

The brilliance of this was that I lived in an Irish neighborhood with fifty two bars within walking distance. In a few hours, I could earn more money than my father earned in a day as a sanitation worker for the city, and for a twelve year old, it was tax free and pure profit.

I had my own box and all supplies in one day, and after a week or so I had a route picked out that maximized my revenue. All I had to do was to avoid any of the bars that my father might frequent on his garbage truck route. My father would not have appreciated it if any one thought that his kid was shining shoes in bars. My mother always felt that there was no shame in earning an honest living.

My business was successful and growing. I knew the bars that already had neighborhood kids working them and knew when to avoid them. Instead of charging fifty cents as some of my competition were doing, I charged fifteen cents and always got at least a quarter and sometimes half a buck for a good job. Occasionally I would get a buck and be told to keep the change.

One trip over to the Bronx, due to my neighborhood running cold that day, gave me an experience that I remember clearly to this day. After shining the shoes for a fairly inebriated man who had a shady looking woman hanging on his barstool, he handed me a one hundred dollar bill. The woman, being quite a bit more worldly than I, snatched the bill from me and replaced it with a single. I'm pretty sure that he never saw that hundred again. If I was sharper, and faster to size up the situation, I would have dropped my box, which was probably worth about six or seven bucks, and ran like hell with my payment. Lesson learned!

All in all my business was doing well and I was profiting nicely. I was able to afford anything that I needed without having to ask anyone for money. I bought a great set of walkie talkies, a banana seat for my bike, and any candy that suited my fancy. I developed a taste for chocolate covered raspberry jellies and on the way home one day I stopped in a candy store and purchased their whole display box which may have held as many as a gross of them. I ate them till I was sick and never had another for years.

In an attempt to maximize my earnings I would start a bit earlier in the day and catch two rounds before nine pm. At nine the Daily News hit the news stand and I would use some of my profit to purchase newspapers to sell for a last shot at the bars.

Life was good. My career was rock n' rolling and I was in the money. Good, honest money which gave me all the freedom that a kid could handle.

A short time before that, I had built my bicycle from scraps from the sanitation yard. Now it was updated with all the accessories that were available from the neighborhood bike shop. I had ram handle bars, streamers, a great bell, and a bag of balloons to tie to the frame to rub against the spokes making the loudest noise possible. It put the old baseball card on the spokes trick to shame. As I said, life was good!

And then came desert boots. Desert boots were hush puppy, suede type shoes which became all the rage in the 1960's and didn't need polishing. They caught on faster than anything I had ever witnessed.

For years, any man worth his salt, wore leather shoes. It was the sign of a gentleman to have clean, polished shoes. No matter what you worked in, when you got home from work you changed into shiny shoes before heading to the bar to socialize, it was tradition. It was that way back in Ireland. It had always been that way. One didn't go to the bar with work boots, sneakers, sandals, or any other un-gentlemanly footwear. And then along came desert boots.

They came on like a storm. They broke all tradition and opened the way for sneakers and whatever else anyone decided was good enough to drink in. My world crashed. None of the new shoes required polishing and within a few months everyone was wearing them.

The revelation that my business was history and that my life as a carefree, independent, successful businessman was ending abruptly became painfully clear. I knew that I would have to join the corporate world and take a job in a delicatessen.

I did try a few other business ventures such as collecting soda bottles for the deposits. Being the super's son, I pulled the ropes and that gave me access to a fairly large amount of bottles.

Pulling the ropes meant that I operated the dumbwaiters in my building. My building had forty five families and each apartment had a dumbwaiter which I sent up from the basement, around five o'clock each evening, to the different apartments to collect the garbage from the tenants. I would ring each apartment's buzzer and send a cart up a dumbwaiter shaft to each apartment by pulling the attached ropes. It was pretty cool. I would pull the dumbwaiter cart to the fifth floor of each shaft where the tenant would open their dumbwaiter door and put their garbage on the cart that I would then lower to the next apartment down until I had all five apartments done on that row. There were nine dumbwaiter shafts in my building.

As I emptied the garbage from each full dumbwaiter into the burlap sacks to take to the street for the garbage pick up by the sanitation department, I could set aside the empty bottles that the tenants were too lazy to take back to the store for the deposit refund. Small bottles were worth two cents and the quart bottles were worth a nickel.

This became a pretty good source of income to help replace the lost revenue of my failed shoeshine business.

Tragedy struck again. My neighborhood only had three sources for returning bottles and I dried all of them up rather quickly. I guess that the soda companies didn't provide incentives for the grocery stores to handle the returned bottles and each of the stores put me off limits because I returned bottles a wagon full at a time. They claimed that my bottles took up all of their storage space.

At thirteen years old I didn't own a car so my world was limited to my neighborhood and my wagon could only hold so many bottles per trip.

Extra help to keep the bottles on the wagon and to protect them from being stolen while in other parts of the neighborhood meant splitting the profit and there just wasn't that much profit at two cents for small bottles and a nickel for the quart size.

I eventually did join the corporate world and took my place as a clerk/stockboy/cleanerupper/sandwichmaker at the deli that had refused to continue to take my bottles. How's that for selling out to the establishment?

If gentlemen still wore dress shoes I could have had my own shoeshine stand by now.

Did the Media Purposely Crush Our Economy?

C ould an ordinary person draw the conclusion that the media purposely played a significant part in damaging the US economy to influence a political election?

A fair assumption is that the majority of media personnel are liberal by nature and would prefer a more liberal government. Because the mainstream media is still the major source of influence for the American public they are in a key position to sway votes. From the news broadcasts, to late night shows, to Saturday Night Live, media has the access to influence.

Even with this unbalanced edge to present a one sided point of view it has not been enough to completely take over the government. For eight years, the big prize has eluded them. This time they were not taking anymore chances. The strong point of the Bush Administration has been the ability to hold off an impending recession and maintain a strong economy. People were employed, and buying cars and other big ticket items.

It appears that the press has begun amplifying the normal downturns of the economy to spook the public. By sabotaging public confidence they have convinced the US voters that their status has tumbled and that only a CHANGE can solve the problem.

A short time later the Democratic candidates ran on a CHANGE platform which had been pre-laid by the media.

Most reports of Wall Street downturns are now reported as 'catastrophic' and 'the worst since the Great Depression', to crush consumer confidence and fulfill their self fulfilled prophesy of destroying our economy for their purpose of the greater good.

The strength of this country has always been in the balance between Conservatives and Liberals. Each side is kept in check by the other and this allows new ideas from each to be tabled and hopefully, the best ideas will go forward.

Neither side has been effective by itself. The House and Senate are both controlled by the Democrats and neither has been successful so far. The prior House and Senate were Republican controlled and were also worthless. For the Media to attempt to flip our total government Liberal and remove any balance at all could be disastrous.

My question is: what are they really willing to do to our country to accomplish their goal, and can we recover from the damage they inflict?

Post script

A short while after writing this, it became clear to me that they were willing to crush our economy and destroy public confidence. Wall Street, banking, and the auto industry succumbed to the sabotage and the rest is history. Boy, did I see this one coming!

Dissatisfied Immigrants

As an ordinary man I am often amazed at the desire of European immigrants to change America. People such as Arianna Huffington and George Soros emigrated to the United States to partake in the greatness of America. They achieved great success and then desire to change America. They go so far as to use their wealth and power, attained through our American environment, to force their desired changes to American government and society. Their wealth and influence are used to heavily influence voters to CHANGE the status quo. They become zealots in their distain of America as it is.

If the desired change is to resemble a European model, then why aren't they living in Europe enjoying the desired environment?

Just as amazing to me is how these people can control huge segments of our population. Their followers are dedicated to fulfilling the desires of these hard left leaning fanatics. They make it chic to hate America as it is and somehow stir the pot of dissent even though the lawmakers are already Democratic in majority. They have been able to convince their followers that the president is the lawmaker instead of congress.

In general, I favor two opposing parties to provide the necessary balance for a healthy America but I resent foreigners attempting to influence the balance.

Why is it so attractive to follow these foreigners who have proven the ability of the American system to provide advancement opportunities to anyone willing to take risks and work hard when this is precisely what they are attempting to change.

If the desire is for a more balanced and socialistic society then why haven't these people donated all of their fortunes beyond normal comforts to the downtrodden.

Lead by example and maybe I'd also become a convert.

$1.35 an Hour

My mother gave me great advice. Move faster than everyone else, always carry something in your hand, and stay busy. This was brilliant advice.

I had been complaining about my job at the deli. At fourteen years old every problem at work seems monumental.

I was working Al's Deli, a small German delicatessen in uptown Manhattan and Al was an old German who slept on a cot in the back room of the store during the week so as not to have to drive home to Long Island except on Sundays. It carried the staples, from bread, milk, soda, some canned goods and potatoes, to cold cuts, salads and sandwiches. All tallies were added up on the paperbags that the goods were placed in. The cash register simply took the total. I can still out add any Burger King cashier in the country.

Al made the potato salads and cooked the meats for the cold cuts and woke up several times during the day to make sure that John and I weren't loafing.

John was an older man who probably weighed in at 120 pounds. Al allowed him a case of beer a day to keep him employed at minimum wage. For each can he drank from his allotment, he drank another can, crushed the can, and placed it behind the paperbags so he could sneak them out with the trash at night.

After a while I figured out that Al probably knew about the extra case of beer but that for the extra three or four bucks a day he had a grown man working for minimum wage.

The daily routine was comical. John arrived late every morning and was crabby as hell. After a few beers he was great. The customers loved John in the afternoon. By evening he was drunk on his butt and arguing with the customers. This went on for years till John finally turned yellow and died.

As we worked together for those few years, the concern that John and I had was Al waking up. Al would wake up unexpectedly and come up front to check on the store. Probably to make sure that John didn't drink too much too early and scare too many customers away.

As he snuck up front; if you were standing still you got the same lecture. "Vot, are you crazy? For a dolla doity five an hour you stand there? Dust the shelves! Rotate the stock!" He did not want to hear that the stock was already rotated and if I did it again I'd be placing the new stock up front. Very frustrating at fourteen!

That's when my mother's advice came in. I never did any more work than normal (there was no more productive work that could be done) but I set a mirror by the soda cases that let me see when Al was awake and I kept the duster in my hand throughout the day so that I could look busy whenever Al was around. Al's complaints diminished and I was permitted to take a pint of Hagen Daz ice cream home each night as I closed up. What a great life!

My mother had told me that if you are waiting tables, fill your salt and pepper shakers continuously and swap them from table to table so that you are always the busiest waiter. The boss always loves a busy worker, and so do the customers. Even in mundane jobs it is wise to move faster than your coworkers, stay busy, and carry something in your hand. No one wants to interrupt a busy worker to do trivial tasks. Brilliant woman!

Even the Asian Kids Failed

Talk about reinforcement of a bitch that I have espoused for years, my daughter, in an attempt to rationalize failing a chemistry test, opened her defense with, "even the Asian kids failed . . ."

My obvious response was, "What do you mean, even the Asian kids failed? What the heck does that have to do with you? Do you believe that you are naturally inferior to Asian kids?" Her response was, "Yeah!"

She did add that there is a 'white kid' who plays baseball and may become the class valor victorian. What a unique situation! At least she has one hero who has broken the glass ceiling!

Is this the same across the whole country? Do these Asian kids work so hard that they have absolutely taken every prestigious position in every school? Are they genetically superior or are their work ethics better? Do their families expect more from them then non-Asian families do? Have we dumbed down our standards to such a degree that 'excellence' is no challenge to a 'normal' kid from outside our culture? What gives?

When the kids believe that there is a hierarchy and they have accepted their position in it, that tells me that the battle will be a tough one.

I have discussed this with my kids throughout their lives and still find out that it does not really sink in. A ten minute conversation with dad every few weeks does not override eight hours in school, hours with friends who share the hierarchy theory, and TV.

I can see the challenges of being a Caucasian family in today's society and seeing the results of a child accepting a position lower than I would expect them to accept.

How about Black families? How many Black kids would be 'exceptional' except for the unfortunate fact that they have accepted a lower standard and work hard every day to live down to it? Why do kids accept this theory and why can't we motivate our kids like the Asian families do? This is probably where I should include the disclaimer that: this does not apply to all situations, all families, nor every kid, and any semblance to bigotry in any negative connotation is purely a misinterpretation on the part of the reader and not the intention of the author.

I don't believe that it necessarily requires more money for schools because Asian kids excel at my kid's schools and I'm certain that they excel in any school they attend throughout America.

I also surmise that teachers believe in their souls that there is a hierarchy and inherently promote the performers. Most new teachers have recently graduated college and have also lived this experience. From my vantage point it seems that there are relatively few Asian teachers in grade schools and high schools. Universities, on the other hand, seem to have a larger presence of Asian professors. Might this also support this theory?

To end on a positive note – if the Asian kids fail a test, you can believe that the test will be re-given.

Everything's Fixed

I had a friend who owned a Dairy Queen a number of years ago. They had a contest with prizes ranging from free ice cream to a vacation in the Caribbean. I asked him what my chances were to win a prize if I filled out an entry form. He said I should fill out a form and I could have the bike but the trip was already spoken for. That was sure an eye opener.

Once, as an Air Force recruiter I had a young female recruit who came to see me about getting out of her delayed enlistment contract. Her boyfriend worked at McDonalds and was bringing home bags of tear open prize tickets at night. They sat around each evening opening the tickets and finally hit a $10,000 ticket. Being an employee, he couldn't collect the prize so she claimed it. With her half of the prize money she decided that she no longer needed a job so the commitment to the Air Force was off.

She gave a great description of the TV filming of the awarding of the check. She was told to pick her favorite McDonalds meal. As it was arranged attractively on a McDonald's table it was sprayed with a water bottle to have it look its best for the camera and she was told to jump up and down screaming 'I won, I won'. She said that when the filming was over the meal was hers for free but it was two hours old and still wet.

State lotteries have been taking a few hits. Massachusetts had been accused a couple of times of fixing the drawings by weighting the numbered balls.

It seems to me that if they fixed it to pull the same numbers that I would have picked, then I would at least have won half of a prize that I wouldn't have had a chance to win if I had picked different numbers.

How's that for a run on sentence!

Today, the problem seems to be state scratch tickets being sold after the prizes have already been won. Out of all the scratch ticket programs in all the states how many millions have been spent without a chance of winning the big prize? To prevent this, a player would have to get to a computer to check each scratch ticket game before making a purchase which is normally made impromptu at the check out counter.

From sports to stocks, one must assume that everything is fixed and simply hope that your pick is the same as the fixer had picked.

This free bit of insight will provide you many benefits. You will no longer waste time trying to figure out the best team, the best stock pick, the smartest scratch ticket game to play, or the luckiest numbers for the lotto. You will also have an excuse to fail when your team loses, your horse finishes last, or your stocks drop.

Please enjoy the extra time I've freed up for your life and the stress reduction I've provided you.

Forget Convention

Where the hell is Black Jack Pershing? As the European nations were fighting WWI as a war of attrition, as per the nineteenth century model, the death toll was phenomenal because men were now marching into weapons which could kill many more men then the muskets which were in use when the tactics were devised.

Thank God Pershing came along to decide that American lives were not going to be lost at that rate just to follow convention. By the way, we won that war!

Our Civil War began on the battle fields emulating French protocol. It cost so many lives that the rules had to change or the North would have simply outlasted the South in very quick time. Creative adaptation by the Southern generals almost kicked Northern butt. Conventional West Point training cost each side a hundred thousand lives unnecessarily. It took five years for Northern generals to adapt. They adapted and won that war.

Our Revolutionary War pitted a better equipped, better manned, and better trained British army and navy against a ragtag army of Colonials who lost most of the conventional battles but kicked British ass when tactics were changed to guerrilla warfare.

Reading British accounts of the same war shows quite a different opinion of American tactics. It sounds more like our present opinion of insurgent tactics in Iraq. We defeated the British. We're not defeating the insurgents.

In these cases, the desire for convention produced catastrophic results. Countless lives were lost due to the failure to adapt, the failure to blow off popular opinion, the failure to blow off the conventional press. Decisions to follow convention should always be made by the man who has his son on the front line.

The new guerrilla tactics have been adapted by a clever enemy to include the utilization of all weapons available, including American politicians with personal agendas, the American liberal press, and the knowledge that the American military will fight a conventional war till so many of our kid's lives are wasted that the public will lose its will to continue.

It happened in Viet Nam and it's happening in Iraq. Either war could have been won in three months. We chose not to win 'at any cost'.

If a mission is important enough to draw us to war, it should be important enough to win 'at any cost'. 'At any cost' means, till every bomb we own is spent, till every aircraft is lost, till every Navy asset is spent, and THEN the loss of American soldiers.

That concept goes against convention but thus far, we haven't won any conventional wars.

Get In the Groove

B eing a huge music fan, I always pay attention whenever I hear it. From live performances to the radio, it never just exists in the background like Musak may do for many people; I listen to it.

More often than people know, music is affecting them. It is used to slow down or speed up shoppers in stores. It's used to calm people in anxious situations. It is used in convalescent homes where nostalgic music is played to add comfort to the elderly patients.

It can get a party going or turn a dull bar into a popular hang out. It can even get church attendance up and keep more people awake in the pews. It's one of the greatest gifts bestowed on us.

There is a certain magic to music; some call it the groove. I saw it in church a short while ago. A young kid playing the guitar was kind of hanging in there for most of the songs till he hit that one song where he caught the groove. From that point on he had more body English than a Haitian Voodoo revival. That church band clicked and that was the song that did it for him.

You can see it in a concert when Wynton Marsalis steps forward and lights up the audience with a killer solo. You could feel it when Cream toured and Clapton, Bruce, and Baker hit the groove and three pieces filled a stadium.

You feel it occasionally when you watch one of the talent shows on TV and one singer has the audience on their feet. You know they're in the groove because the hair stands up on your arms.

The groove is there when two young singers hit their first vocal harmony and all of a sudden, to them at least, that song sounds like the record.

The groove is there when you hear a Puerto Rican percussionist tapping out a rhythm then he's joined by another and another and they just sync. Each is playing off the heartbeat of the other and when it's working, it's magical. Fifty people standing around the stoop listening can feel the groove when it's there. It sucks you in.

Get Out From Under My Sink

I learned a great lesson about kids from a Co-worker of mine. Years ago, before I had kids of my own, I had a definite intolerance for undisciplined kids. As friends with children would visit, it drove me nuts when they would pull the items from under my sink or drip their drinks on my floor. It was always uncomfortable when the parents permitted the destruction of my home. It got to the point where I didn't want the friends to visit if I had to endure their kids. And then along comes Larry.

Larry was an intolerant Vermont boy who had no patience for kids and never failed to voice that opinion. The unexpected result was that the kids loved him. The more that he would yell, the more they loved him. Maybe it was because he offered the first discipline that some of these spoiled brats had ever experienced.

The parents never seemed to say much. Maybe they thought that he was only kidding or maybe they were glad that someone had finally gotten their kids to behave, which may have offered hope to parents who had read too many books by 'professionals' and had decided that their kids were broken.

Let a kid go under Larry's sink and all hell broke loose, "get out from under my sink before I feed you to my dogs!". The kids got out from under his sink. "What are you doing with a drink on my couch? Are you nuts?!" It always worked and the kids always loved him.

Rather than ban kids from my house, the 'Larry' approach has made kids more palatable. Even my own kids were manageable enough to keep. I don't think that I have offended too many parents and if I did,

I can rationalize it enough in my own mind to believe that if they had raised their kids right in the first place, I wouldn't have had to yell.

Half a lifetime later the technique still works. As many adults are intimidated by unruly kids and harbor a resentment which can affect their friendship with the parents because they are afraid to hurt someone's feelings by applying the discipline required to stop a child from damaging property, I don't have that problem.

Harmonies

Birds may have this singing thing down but people have the edge on harmonies. I figure that harmonies must be what separates us from the animals.

Harmonies are magic; two, three, four, or more part harmonies. The two part, like Simon and Garfunkel made great songs even better and allowed songs with brilliant lyrics to sell to more audience.

Two part harmonies from artists like the Everly Brothers made any song a big seller. It was their trademark. Some vocalists just belong together, like Sara Evans and Adam Levine. Sometimes there's a magic that occurs when the right voices and personalities combine.

To a musical theorist, a harmony is obtained simply by multiplying the base note (not to be confused with the *bass* note) frequency by 1.5 to gain the fifth. There has long been a search for the 'perfect fifth' but that's a whole other story. A great good harmonizer can feel the fifth without any math involved. Thank God!

Some believe that sibling harmonies, such as the Bee Gees, or the Andrew Sisters are the best. They usually are, but every once in a while a right combination of vocalists hits and it's golden.

It's not always the quality of the voices. Sometimes it's just the chord combinations such as the Beach Boy harmonies, stolen from Jan and Dean, and arranged by Brian Wilson, which are killer to listen to, even when the individual voices are not outstanding.

It was more than just their falsettos that drove the sound. The intricate four part combinations became their trademark.

The Four Seasons' falsetto driven harmonies were distinctly different from the Beach Boys sound and were strong enough to set the mode all the way through the 1960's till, and through, the disco era. The power that they pumped into the top end took the Philadelphia sound of the 50's to the zenith.

The Eagles understood vocal blends and turned great songs, which could have sold as single voice hits, into classics which are as great to listen to live as they are on the albums. Not many bands can duplicate their studio sound on a live stage. I guess that thirty plus years of harmonizing together helps.

When bands form, vocalists can sometimes find their parts immediately and sometimes they can't. Some work forever to try to duplicate harmonies from other bands and some just feel what's needed right away. They meld and blend and can automatically anticipate each other's direction. They can feel what should be there and provide it. Some simply provide the fifth, seventh, or octave each time but the true professional feels what is needed for every song and plays off the other vocalists.

I always liked Beatles harmonies in that every song was different. Voices were used to provide orchestration when they were simply a four piece band, and they still used orchestrated harmonies when the songs had actual instrument orchestration. From 'Meet the Beatles' to 'Let it Be' they never disappoint.

The Stones, on the other hand, built their sound more around Jagger as a solo vocalist and never impressed me with harmonies. I always leaned more toward the Beatles.

Motown built an industry on three and four part harmonies and controlled the charts for decades with Berry Gordy and Smokey Robinson pushing harmony driven tunes making the Temptations, The Four Tops, The Miracles, and The Supremes household names since the 1960's.

Regardless of the genre, the one common denominator to most of my favorites is harmony.

Hold This for Me

'Hold this for me'. How would this play in a psychology class? The words 'for me' set a unique air in a sentence.

A young hairdresser used these words a short while ago and it caught my attention. I have since, heard them used many times; usually by waitresses or other service providers. It is becoming more common for telephone receptionists to say, "Please hold for me", when taking a call. When I first heard it I wondered how the interaction would be addressed in the psychology books.

Adding 'for me' to a request adjusts the roles of the persons involved. A teacher may say, "Do this for me." to a young student and it sets a certain tone. It says that the teacher is in a superior position to the subordinate student, and is allowing that student the privilege of doing the teacher a favor.

In the same vein, when a hairdresser or waitress adds 'for me' to a request, it raises the status of their position at that moment. By not addressing the issue, the patron accepts a subordinate position.

I do wonder how many times this has affected the gratuity provided because the patron was subconsciously offended by this psychological placement to the inferior position.

The service provider may have found a way to momentarily raise their status in that interaction, but, is it worth a reduced tip when you are primarily working for tips.

On one hand, what does it matter, as long as it adds a bit of an ego boost to a person in an otherwise thankless job?

On the other hand, what the hell am I even noticing this stuff for?

Home Owner's Insurance

I learned a lot about home owner's insurance during the past few years. One thing is, I pay an awful lot of money for the protection.

A short while ago I called to make a claim after an upstairs water spill damaged the downstairs ceiling. Fortunately, the adjuster was a friend of a friend and he informed me that after my deduction and the potential increase in premiums it would be much more economical for me to cover the repairs myself; which I did.

Confirming my opinion, I spoke with my dog's vet and listened to his tale of whoa about his homeowner's insurance. It seems that he had three items looked at by an adjuster. Choosing not to make a claim on two of them, he claimed on one and the insurance company paid $247 after deductibles.

This turned out to be a bad mistake. Three contacts assigned a 'chronic' tag to his policy and his premiums skyrocketed. To make it worse, the 'chronic' tag is shared among other insurance companies and he has paid for that $247 many times over.

His question was, why wasn't he informed of the repercussions of three contacts. It is fairly common knowledge regarding inquiries on your credit bureau affecting your score.

Instances, such as these, which can be extremely costly to an unsuspecting consumer should be presented to the person before the adverse action is applied. Most people have only minor contact with insurance companies, as well as credit bureaus, and should not be expected to know the idiosyncrasies and dire consequences of violating their secret codes.

With all the consumer protection advocates out there, the homeowner's insurance companies may have remained the most successful at avoiding their scrutiny.

How Important Are Teachers?

It seems that the most impressive teachings come during grade school where a young mind is like a sponge.

Most adults seem to remember more trivia from that period of their lives than any other. It's where you learn your basic math, English, and history. These are the building blocks for all future success. It's where you learn about '1492' and a million other tidbits which stay with you for the rest of your life. Hell, they make TV shows about what you learned in the fifth grade.

Many successful adults can trace their success back to specific teacher who went above and beyond the norm.

It can't be about the money that a teacher is paid or the Catholic school kids wouldn't be as successful as they always seem to be. It's about the motivation of the teacher.

If you ever think that these people are not important to your child's welfare – you're nuts. These people have more direct contact with our kids than most parents can ever have. For six, or more, hours per day they have them as a captive audience. I don't know many parents who see their kids for that many consecutive hours in a day unless they sleep in the same room.

Thinking back to my own teachers in grade school, each one still seems impressive to me. In the business world today I meet a good number of teachers and many don't seem quite as impressive as what I remember teachers to be. Many wouldn't pass a job interview due to their speaking skills and I pray that they aren't teaching our children to speak in the same manner.

A number of teachers that I have dealt with are not aware that 60 months equals 5 years – not 6. I have personally experienced this on more than one occasion.

What are the reasons for the diminution of the quality of so many teachers? Although many teachers are definitely underpaid, in a one on one conversation, the more common complaint is about the temperament of the student, which is aggravated by the parent (singular), and augmented by the lack of backing from the school administration.

To elaborate, it is common knowledge that many kids are simply punks. There have always been punks but they were often offset by a cooperating and sympathetic set of parents. I still remember well the threat of 'wait till your father finds out'; and it was quite a threat. I wasn't just afraid of the ruler across the hand in school; the repercussion that night gave second thoughts to playing the fool in class. In retrospect, it isn't a bad process when applied without abuse.

Compounding the lack of respect for a teacher by the student and his parent is the political concern of the administration to appease the parent regardless of the damage done to the student and the teacher.

To a teacher there are two distinctly different classifications of principals. The first, and preferred, is the principal who progressed through the ranks from teacher to principal. This person has the empathy to not blindly side with the parent against the teacher simply to protect their job security.

The second, and blithe on most teachers, is the professional administrator who always sides with the parent against the teacher. Never having been a teacher and facing a threatening punk, there is no compassion for the teacher. To a teacher this is every bit as noteworthy as the lack of pay.

How will today's teachers ever achieve the results achieved by teachers of the past?

How Serious is the Gas Crisis?

How serious is the gas crisis? It depends on who it is affecting. Undoubtedly, many are making fortunes from it. That extra money being spent by consumers is getting quite a lot of people very rich. One thing that is understood by anyone with a brain is that, in all production, from food to fuel, the middle man makes the money: traders, speculators, packagers, distributors, and the guy who puts it in your possession.

As much as the consumer suffers, the consumer has very little say except in boycotting the product (impossible) or electing representatives who will fight the fight (impossible). This is impossible because, remember, no matter how crooked Congress is, my representative is the only honest one. And, if he, or she, is not honest, at least they are bringing the goods back to my district.

American consumers have no say in the gas crisis and it is not yet considered serious enough for Congress, or the President to enact changes.

I will know when it hits the breaking point. When it does, NASA will be re-missioned to solve the energy quagmire.

The top American scientists and physicists will put space on a back burner and will develop the proper batteries, motors, and whatever the future brings to replace current power sources which are not efficient enough to be affordable to the American consumer who has to afford gasoline as the power source.

NASA had been responsible for so many breakthroughs and new inventions, as when under the gun to put a man on the moon, that today we enjoy digital technology, kidney dialysis machines, CAT scans, and thousands of other NASA byproducts which we take for granted. When the pressure was on – NASA performed.

Why isn't the pressure on now? We are now completely dependent on Japanese innovation to provide solutions.

Kennedy motivated a program which revolutionized technology. Why was Kennedy a better motivator than Bush or Obama? Kennedy was concerned about the Soviets controlling space and placing weapons in space which would threaten the US. He commanded NASA to develop a space program and put a man on the moon by the end of the decade and it was done. The guy cared, and acted. No one today cares, or acts. Do not listen to the rhetoric, watch the commands. No one is commanding a solution. In the mean time, pray for the Japanese to save us.

Hum Vee 12/10/04

This is a piece that I wrote to pass around to friends to generate letters to their representatives. At the time, the debate was on the modification of HumVees to protect our troops who were coming home mangled due to IEDs becoming the weapon of choice by Iraqis.

American troop safety is one of the highest priorities in my world. These heroes, who are prepared to lay it all on the line for us, are one of the few things in the world that can choke me up.

The subject of the hour seems to be the protection of our troops in Iraq while riding in HumVees. My belief as to why they are so poorly armored is this: the vehicles were lightly armored because they were not designed to operate under the present conditions. And, we were not supposed to be there this long so why change the configuration for a temporary use and improperly configure for future use.

Cost effectiveness overrode troop safety. The troops are attempting to modify their vehicles in the field to protect their lives. These field modifications are necessary but appear to be temporary fixes which are making the vehicles worthless for future use.

I believe the proper fix is *not* to replate all new vehicles which will render them inadequate for the Pentagon's perception of the lighter, faster vehicle for future wars, but to modify all new vehicles with detachable armor plates (maybe even Kevlar type materials) to snap on for combat use and snap off for non-combat and shipping.

If this is a feasible fix – what would it take to DO IT NOW? What is a soldier's legs, arms, or life worth compared to following proper contract etiquette?

If this makes sense please forward it to as many people as possible till it reaches a decision maker. God Bless Our Troops.

Human Strength

M y belief is that humans are, by nature, much stronger than manifested today. The psychological problems of so many people may be brought on by the acceptance that the human psyche is fragile. Maybe too much sensitivity training!

For a bazillion years lions had been stealing babies from mothers and eating them. Although crushed, for sure, at the time, there were no support groups, nor antidepressants. There was no alternative. Mom was forced to adapt to tragedy to keep the human race alive.

As the effects of the cruelty of nature have been reduced through the centuries, we are still the same human beings. The strength that is needed to maintain existence in spite of tragedy is still in there. It has just been masked by exposure to television.

The death of a college student brings psychological counselors out of the woodwork. The students are convinced that help must be accepted to survive the ordeal

These same kids, when placed in a war zone, perform their duties heroically. Without confirmation of how bad the situation is to their psyche a soldier will normally adapt and overcome[3].

People who suffered through concentration camps and gulags for years at a time had witnessed countless deaths of family and friends and relied on family, friends, and inner strength to survive. Today, it is a paid crisis counselor that is needed.

---

[3] There may always be some exceptions as there is a breaking point for anyone. Some veterans with extreme battle exposure exhibit post traumatic stress.

An athlete collapsing on the field can cause the whole team to require crisis counseling. With all the psych majors graduating I guess they need to stay employed.

If the message to people today is that we cannot handle tragedy without some higher agency handling our psychological recovery, how can we survive as our ancestors did, and as the people of the third world do on a daily basis? By forcing a dependency on sources outside ourselves and our family we may be becoming too fragile to survive in a real world.

I Don't Speak the Language

I spoke with my mother in law who still lives in uptown Manhattan. She's a die-hard New Yorker who will never leave her apartment. She's been there for half a century and could have bought the building for what she's paid in rent.

The subject of her health came up and she mentioned that she had a doctor's appointment coming soon. Navigating the three flights of stairs is enough of a challenge, but arranging transportation to the hospital for her appointment is becoming increasingly trying – and costly. I recommended that she look into the hospital transport service that is provided.

She feels that the reason she has not been able to take advantage of this is because she does not speak enough Spanish to make the arrangements.

A while ago she lost her cable and was unable to get to an English speaking rep. The people assigned to her area are almost exclusively Spanish speakers. Trying to assist from out of state I eventually called to a New Jersey tech number and was able to arrange for an English speaking tech to call her. For a woman who still uses a rotary dial phone, a cable tech who speaks fluent English is a must.

It's a very uncomfortable feeling for a widow who has lived her life as a typical American woman to have to shop in a tienda instead of a supermarket or to sit in a beauty parlor where all conversation, including the TV, is in Spanish.

Being born and raised in America she assumed that English would be her language and that she would always fit in. Wrong!

Putting aside the crime situation in her area, where adults fear walking alone in the streets, many visitors remark on how exotic the neighborhoods have become. The lively Latin music doesn't seem to thrill my mother in law at two o'clock in the morning.

To the unaffected observer the new culture is warmly welcomed. To the displaced expatriate who happens to be living in the same neighborhood for fifty years, the desire is for the new cultures to meld into the American culture as they had for 200 years. The mandate today is to adjust to the new immigrants' language and culture or leave. At ninety one years of age that's a tough decision.

I Don't Want My Home Value to Rise

A s homes in my area began selling for higher and higher prices
my wife was thrilled to think that our home's value was
skyrocketing. As a matter of fact, most people that I speak with were
excited that their property values have doubled in the past few years
even though many have tapered off or even dropped a bit.

The first question I ask in such a conversation is: do you anticipate
selling your home? If not, why the hell do you want your property
value to rise when your property taxes are directly correlated to it?
The only one making out at this stage, for a family who remains in
their home, is the tax man.

If one was to sell at the inflated value, the profit would be attractive
only if the seller plans to rent his next home. To buy at this point
simply places you in an inflated market with higher mortgage costs
and higher taxes.

I have rarely experienced a case of property taxes diminishing due
to property values dropping. I hope that some are enjoying a reduction
of taxes but I have yet to enjoy it.

It's a funny balance between interest rates and property values.
When rates were at ridiculous levels, when the prime was in the
teens, home prices were low because it was assumed that a home
mortgage could not be more than a wage earner can afford, for obvious
reasons.

At this point property values were low but money was being made
by banks and the fed. That was the time for cash buyers to clean up.

Private lenders who did not have to borrow from the fed also stood to capitalize.

When Carter left office and the prime approached single digits again property values jumped. My house value at that time rose 25% within a year. I thought that was great because I sold my home and did not need to purchase again.

It seems that mortgage amounts stayed stable for a while but it was simply the prices rising to make up for the lower rates. God forbid that the buyers would actually enjoy lower payments.

I guess the bottom line is: buy a home that you plan to stay in and raise your family in. The external factors can do what they will, but won't affect you if you purchased the right house.

I'll Take Both

Years ago I heard a great story to emphasize the importance of maintaining integrity when dealing with customers. It was told at a conference for Air Force recruiters. The story was impressive enough for me to remember it all these years later and I have passed it on many times. I have found that the need for integrity in dealings, transcends business and is every bit as important in family and social interactions.

In the business world there are certain understandings when negotiations take place. Some of these techniques are ancient and are still practiced in various forms today. For example: when two ancient Egyptians negotiated the sale of a camel, a hundred white lies were exchanged. Sahib would tell Emil that he only possessed five sheckles when he indeed had seven. Emil would claim that the camel could walk ten days in the desert and could father twenty camels a month, when in fact, the camel may have been a bit older than he appeared and was actually gay. This had been the standard of negotiations forever.

My integrity story was told to New York recruiters and the scenario was perfect. I have never heard it again and so I lay claim to it.

The story takes place in the outdoor market of New York, many years ago. Mrs. Sullivan approaches the chicken salesman at the end of the day and announces that she is having some special guests over, on short notice, for dinner and is in need of a chicken.

The chicken salesman reaches into his tub of ice and feels around only to find that he has just one chicken left in the tub. Upon pulling it out he says, "that will be thirty five cents."

Mrs. Sullivan exclaims that they will be very special guests and that she would like a larger chicken.

Pushing the chicken back into the tub of ice, he shakes it around and pulls it back out and says, "this one will be fifty cents". Mrs. Sullivan retorted, "thank you, I'll take them both."

After sinking in for a minute, the parable says a lot. It is clever and funny on the surface but opens the door for great discussion. Most of all, it makes the point.

Insurance

For a normal working family insurance is a killer. Life insurance can be about $400 per month. Car insurance for two adults and one teenage drive, about $200 per month. Home insurance, about $100 per month. Health and dental coverage, another $100 to $600.

Many also have flood, vision, rental, or PMI for mortgage protection for the bank.

Some may pay more or less for any particular insurance but the total is probably close for most middle class families.

My old man never *made* as much money as I pay today for insurance.

Irish History

O nce you leave New York or Boston, Irish history becomes tainted by English intervention. Living away from New York it is interesting to hear the common interpretation of the situation in Northern Ireland.

It is normally seen as a religious problem between Catholics and Protestants. It was more advantageous to present it that way by the English because they found empathy in a mostly Protestant American public and government.

For much of American history, there has been ownership and/or influence of our media by the English. The truth is, that in the conflict, religion has never been the basis of the problem.

For most of Irish modern history, Catholics and Protestants had lived side by side in most Irish communities and enjoyed complete harmony. Catholic and Protestant churches were in most of the larger towns. Religion was not an issue.

The most serious problem started with Oliver Cromwell early in the 17th century. To pay debts to his armies and war financers he gave Irish land, farms, homes and factories to his soldiers and creditors.

His war against Ireland was fought as part of the English Civil War which pitted Protestants against Catholics. With Ireland being predominantly Catholic and Cromwell's forces being Protestant; and Cromwell desiring to eradicate Catholics, it was not a promising situation for the Irish.

Irish families were thrown out of their homes and their homes were given to Cromwell's creditors. As these newly homeless families were left to starve, they knew that their possessions were now owned by Protestants.

Catholics were not permitted to live in towns, not permitted to vote, attend Catholic Church, or own land. Everything of value was now owned by Protestants and everything needed by the Catholics had to be purchased from the Protestants.

As the years went by and Catholics again returned to the towns and work places, the differences in the haves and the have-nots was most easily identified by religion.

The resentment was not because of one's religious beliefs but because one religion had dispossessed and oppressed the other.

Many Protestants, through the generations, had realized the truth of their history, and were sympathetic to the Catholics, and understood the ruthlessness of the English. Oddly enough, some of the most famous Irish patriots, such as Wolfe Tone, were Protestants who fought and died for the Irish Cause.

When faced with English oppression the US was able to defeat the British with the help of 3000 miles of ocean, this, unfortunately, was not the case for the Irish.

The remnants of the 'troubles' are present even today. Many of the richest businesses in Ireland are still owned by Protestant families even though Protestants are a small minority of the overall population. Even Guinness is Protestant owned!

It was not until well into the 20th century that Catholics were freely permitted to attend Trinity College, the largest and most famous college in Ireland. English history teaches that Catholics could not attend only because they risked excommunication from the Church. True history shows that Catholics were excluded by English rule.

As Catholics are now permitted to become educated, and Ireland, as part of the European Union, can now trade freely, Ireland is becoming one of the fastest growing success stories in Europe.

With only four million people in the 'free state', one half the population of New York City, Ireland has had quite an impact on some of the most successful nations in the world: the US, Canada, Australia, and New Zealand. Irish immigrants have contributed immensely to their success, producing citizens whose families have gone on to enrich their new homes. People like Ronald Reagan and the Kennedy's have shown the positive legacy of Irish immigration, both Protestant and Catholic.

Italian Food

Italian restaurants seem to opening and closing faster than ever. So many restaurants are doing so well, with one hour waiting lists just to sit down, that it's hard to believe that any restaurant could fail anymore. Makes you believe that all the new homes are being built sans kitchens.

The reason for Italian restaurant failures? Nuveau Italiano! (hope I got that right). Real Italian cooks cook their sauce forever. The ingredients simmer in a pot till every herb, tomato, and seasoning meld together for the perfect smooth, signature sauce.

The new wave Italian cooks expect us to believe that spaghetti sauce has clumps of tomatoes. New sauce has clumps of tomatoes because new cooks are too lazy and cheap to cook their sauce till the tomatoes break down into the proper consistency. Instead of preparing it properly they are trying to convince us that clumpy, semi-cooked sauce is 'authentic Italian'. Thus, one reason for the failures.

Another reason for the failures, in my humble opinion, is the belief that all food should have Mexican seasoning because Mexican seasonings are en vogue. If I want Mexican I'll go Mexican! It seems like much of the Italian foods today taste like they were seasoned with jalapeños and hot sauce. Not my idea of Italian! It has gone so far that delivery pizza today arrives with jalapeños in the box.

And, why do these 'bistro' mentality maggots believe that just because garlic is an Italian seasoning that everything Italian should have huge chunks of garlic permeating every meal. In some restaurants every bite you take crunches pieces of garlic which were not cooked and blended into the sauce but tossed into a semi-cooked, 'get it on the table fast' plate. Thank God I didn't have an Italian grandmother. I'd be awake each night afraid that she'd be rolling over in her grave at what passed for Italian food.

One of my favorite memories is of my time in Cambridge, England. A new Italian restaurant had opened which had a great feel to it. It was below street level and looked like a wine cellar with whitewashed walls, wine barrels, and classic looking tables with red and white checkered table cloths. The owners were from Italy and were hoping to have a successful restaurant such as they had heard about in New York.

After being open for a while the owner was very disappointed with his lack of clientele. Being American, I was looking for anything that resembled Italian food from New York and found myself eating there quite a few times. Many times it wasn't much more than just me and my wife in the restaurant. Eventually, we spent many of our meals conversing with the owner/chef.

He was curious as to why the Italian restaurants were so successful in New York and what he was doing wrong. I told him my observations and recommendations on menu items that would attract the local Americans and eventually, the Cambridge residents. I explained my interpretation of veal parmesan and all my other favorite dishes and offered to be the guinea pig taste tester till he got it right. They had to be some of the best Italian meals of my life. I recommended that restaurant to all of my American friends and probably impressed them with my doggie bags.

Business did pick up and I eventually left the area. I don't believe that I ever ate that well again. It's funny how you travel the world and try to make the rest of the world just like back home.

I've Not Seen It

En vogue speech always fascinates me. Now that the valley girl influence has finally waned it seems like the style has switched to the 'old Irish washerwoman' mode.

The contractions have become different. Instead of 'I haven't seen it'; it has now become 'I've not seen it'. Very 'old Irish washerwoman'! And, as if the 'old Irish washerwoman' hadn't made enough of an impact, she has stolen the word 'yes' from our language. When asked a question such as 'are you going to the party?'; instead if responding 'yes' or 'yes I am', the 'old Irish washerwoman' answer is 'I am'.

Today's responses are 'I am', 'I will', or 'I do'.

Last year's en vogue speech was the 'Bill Clinton strain'. Each New York business woman interviewed on TV struggled to have enough oxygen to speak a normal sentence. It sounded like they were trying to imitate Bill Clinton in his normal speaking voice. It was so prevalent that most people couldn't hear it unless it was pointed out.

The previous fad was to pose every sentence in the form of a question as if to say 'do you follow me?'. The cadence was | | | ↑?, such as 'the sky was ↑ blue?', or 'we went to the ↑ movies?'.

I was listening to an American artist being interviewed on BBC radio and the British DJs were having a ball making fun of her speech pattern. One DJ commented that he had just returned from California and that everyone spoke like that in America.

My retort would have been about the British obsession for the word 'brilliant'. It is used in every description of anything positive, such as; 'his performance was brilliant', 'that was brilliant', or even, 'the meal was brilliant'. 'Brilliant' had nothing to do with luminescence or high intelligence, it simply implies 'very good'.

It has become the most overused adjective in Britain and transcends from the street urchins to the newscasters.

At least in America, you wouldn't ever catch Brian Williams talking like an 'old Irish washerwoman' or like a Bill Clinton wanna be, or following whatever fad is popular that day. I've not heard any of the pros succumb.

Jackson's Setup

I wrote this after an alleged gaffe made by Jesse Jackson as he awaited an interview at FOX studios. The miss-speak, I believed to be intentional to mislead the voters into thinking that he was opposed to Obama. Jackson was supposedly caught off guard by a camera he believed to be off.

My accusation is that Jesse Jackson and the Democratic managers purposely orchestrated the FOX debacle where Jackson misspoke in front of a live camera.

The benefit would be to show the difference between Obama and Jackson in the attitude toward wayward Black fathers. Knowing that the Black voters are already voting nearly 100% for Obama regardless of ANYTHING, the prize is White voters. White voters have already rejected Jackson twice.

This is simply a ploy to lure undecided White voters to Obama by making him appear more palatable by being at odds with Jackson. 'The enemy of my enemy . . . '

I found it too coincidental that this would have occurred at the FOX studio which is enemy territory for democrats. Especially from someone who had misspoke before and has an in-depth knowledge of TV studios.

If you believe that there is at least a possibility of this being true, please pass this on. If you think that this is too far out to be true, just remember the prize: the Presidency of the United States! By Jackson falling on his sword now, there would be a hell of a prize in payback for him and for his Black cause when Obama wins.

John Wants to be on Broadway

As a junior in high school my son toyed with the idea of heading for Broadway. His skill level was pretty impressive but the though of the possibility of quitting school to try to break into Broadway was very disconcerting to me.

I took him and his brother to New York to visit their Grandmother and to take a ride downtown to see the theater district. Coming from the suburbs in Southeast Virginia it was quite an awakening to see the real New York.

From uptown we took the subway to 42nd street. He wanted to drive but I explained that a teenager in New York City would not be traveling by car. As we rode the subway it was amusing to see how obviously out of place these kids were.

As they stared at everything in fear and amazement, every bum and panhandler picked them as an easy mark and one after another approached them for a handout. By the time we left the station at 41st street they were both holding on to my belt.

We walked through the theater district and I pointed out the items which would become an important part of an actor's life. It didn't seem to have that magic that he expected and after a short while he was ready to head back uptown to grandma's apartment.

To ensure that he got a clear picture of life in New York City we took the #10 bus north and rode it to the last stop which is a block from the Apollo Theater.

As the bus made its last stop my boys realized that they were two white kids on 125th street in Harlem, New York City, at eleven o'clock on a Friday night.

Reluctant to get off the bus, they were goaded by the bus driver who said, "Get off my bus. This is the last stop." I pointed out, to my son, that he was actually at the Apollo Theater, one of the most famous theaters in the world and that it may one day become an important part of his life. Under the circumstances, it didn't impress him much. The crowds outside were a bit louder than he would have expected for such a prominent theater.

All the boys wanted to do at that point was to catch a cab back uptown. I explained that eleven pm in Harlem was not exactly an easy time to catch a cab so we would walk to Grandma's. We were on 125th street and needed to walk to 218th street; a good healthy trek for three young men.

As we walked through Harlem and then the Heights, my boys got to experience, first hand, the multi-culturalism of New York City. Through the Heights and past the George Washington Bridge they received full exposure to the Dominican influence on New York City. At midnight in the Heights, as a car followed closely behind the three white guys walking through the wrong neighborhood, my boys got a feel for the real New York; the New York tour that most tourists never take.

Straight up Broadway into Inwood where the Puerto Rican culture makes you feel like you're in San Juan with all the bells and whistles. The music, the bodegas, and the busy streets, even after midnight; the experience of a lifetime for a couple of kids from the suburbs.

At Grandma's apartment I was told that there never was a serious consideration to quit school and head to Broadway. The life of a starving artist was not as attractive as I had misunderstood him to say. I don't think that he has ever returned to New York City.

Juice

What could be better than a cold glass of juice for breakfast? One of the simplest and best tasting drinks in the world; it has been around forever and should have been able to withstand changes for another million years.

Why have the lying, deceitful maggots interfered with the one natural drink left? Thank God there are federal requirements to list ingredients on labels in this country. A fruit juice named 'strawberry banana' may have virtually none of either in the ingredients. Apple juice and grape juice are relatively cheap to produce so the major ingredient in 'strawberry banana' is going to be apple or grape juice with a small trace of strawberry or banana puree to keep the lie at only ninety percent. Additives can somehow make apple and grape juice taste like anything desired if the container shows a nice enough picture to lead you to expect a certain flavor.

The suggestion of the flavor through fraudulent pictures and script does quite a bit to mislead you. If I haven't been told what the flavor is supposed to be, it is sometimes difficult to identify the flavor.

How much cherry juice should be in cherry juice? How much papaya should be in papaya juice? Why does 100% natural grape juice contain corn syrup for sweetness? To a trusting buyer 100% natural grape juice should contain 100% grape juice – period!

That's not all that pisses me off with juice. Why the hell does the manufacturer put artificial calcium in orange juice? If you want calcium, drink milk, eat ice cream, or take a calcium pill. Why would you consume orange juice for calcium? And, if you can't taste the artificial calcium in the juice, you could probably drink Tang and never know the difference. It would be much cheaper.

The latest trick from these deceitful maggots is the 'premium' orange juice sold in a glass container to infer that you can still buy quality – if you can afford it.

As that concept was spoon fed to the consumer, the next step was to put other fruit juices in similar containers at high prices to let the consumer assume that such a costly juice must be 'as advertised'. Bull! Read the ingredients instead of the name on the label. Screwed again!

I had thought that it was agreed upon that juice was to be juice and a deviation was to be titled 'drink' or 'cocktail'. Leave my juice alone.

Kill Switches Change
a Generation

The history of car buying through the generations has been a constantly changing thing. In the car sales business it has been common knowledge that if you know your customer, you'll be successful.

The 'non-rich' seem to buy the most vehicles so I tend to pay the most attention to that market.

The 'well to do' buyers are less desirable as customers because there are fewer of them and they buy fewer cars. Most want something for nothing and are never satisfied by good service. They will often cut corners on warranties then cry when there's a problem.

The 'non-rich' can often be classified best by generation. Fifty or more years ago, buyers put credit integrity much higher on their priority list. A solid home with an on time mortgage payment and a reliable, affordable car was a badge of honor.

As the generations advanced, the priorities changed for the lower income earners to where a home became less important than what you drive because many feel that, 'no one has to see where you live but everybody sees what you drive'. In other words, it's more prestigious to live in a low rent apartment and drive an SUV than to have a nice, affordable home and drive a hooptie.

To get that SUV, it was critical for the younger buyer to tap grandma as a cosigner. Too bad that all the grandmas have been tapped – and 'burned' by the grandkids who never pay their car note even though they killed grandma's credit.

The last few years have produced millions of buyers who drive nothing but 'flash' and pay 20-30% interest rates because that's what the banks can demand to let a dead beat drive.

Dead beats often buy the prestigious looking vehicle then make the first few payments before they realize that the car is taking most of their entertainment budget. By strategically paying, and then not paying, and then hiding the vehicle from the repo man, they can often manage to keep the 'ride' for a year or more.

In response to this trend the dealerships that specialize in that type of buyer have incorporated a kill switch in the vehicle that prevents the engine from restarting if a signal is sent from the dealership.

A special contract is signed between the credit bandit and the dealership which says that the kill switch will be activated upon the first late payment. Although there is quite a bit of legal challenge, the switch is showing up in more and more markets.

Wouldn't it be a great thing if something as simple as this brought buyers around full circle to where responsible credit became the norm.

Kmart, the Loss of an Empire

L ong before ever seeing a Wal-Mart I had always had a Kmart near my home. Kmart had become a household name and had promised to become the power player in American retail. Positioned in many towns and a possessing a strong reputation, the future seemed guaranteed for Kmart.

With the introduction of Wal-Mart to compete town for town against Kmart the battle was on. The battle didn't seem to go well for Kmart, even in the towns where they were already established long before Wal-Mart's arrival.

Although each appeared similar in size and inventory Mal-Mart won out time after time. At this time, the Kmarts that still remain open seem to sit with empty parking lots while Wal-Marts are packed almost 24 hours a day with a new one opening in town after town almost every week.

To solve this mystery I did what Kmart management should have done years ago. I went directly to the experts. I asked my wife "Why would you put up with the crowded parking lot of Wal-Mart when you can buy the same product for the same price at Kmart?" The answer was the same as I received from many ex-Kmart shoppers and the same as I experienced for myself time after time during the last few years.

You can't get out of the store! No matter how many shoppers are in the store, there are always too few checkouts open. The ploy may have been to have the shoppers spend more time in the checkout line so that they would mull over the items posted there and make more purchases. The result was that shoppers elected to shop at Wal-Mart where they could make their purchase and leave.

This has been the case for years now and has killed Kmart. Driving into an empty Kmart parking lot and an empty store at midnight still doesn't let a shopper out as fast as a crowded Wal-Mart at noon on a Saturday. Shoppers avoid Kmart like the plague.

Why couldn't management see this? And what made me decide to write about this at this time?

Today, in Kmart, I had two items to check out and it looked like it was gonna be a long one. It was to the point that I was preparing to put the items back and head for Wal-Mart. No kidding! As I was heading for the door I heard the manager announce that all cashiers needed to head for their stations. A minute later he repeated his order quite a bit more forcefully. I actually heard numerous customers comment audibly. His third announcement was to the point," all cashier to their checkouts NOW!" This brought a very favorable response from the customers. I actually changed my mind and made my purchase. The cashier however, must not have appreciated the manager's announcements and I found her quite rude; making me think that she was not used to being required to do her job.

Maybe management at Kmart has finally learned what the shoppers have known for years.

La La La La La

L a Keisha, La Kenya, LaToya, LaQuinta, LaQuita, LaRonda . . .
Dwayne, Dejon . . .
To the non-black community this is a fairly safe tip-off that the
owner of any name similar to these is African-American. For many
comedians, alluding to this fact has provided fodder for many a joke.

It has been that way forever. Previously, a joke would have began
with, 'Paddy says to Guido . . . ' Today it may be, 'Paddy says to
LaKeisha . . .'. Where the first case inferred an Irishman speaking
to an Italian, the second supposes an Irishman speaking to a Black
woman.

Many would ask why Blacks have begun naming their children
with such unique names. The answer, which I'm not sure that most
moms even realize, is why not? Why should a name pay tribute to
a European saint from a period when Blacks inhabited a completely
different part of the world? Classic European names need not have
any allure to an American Black.

To an Irish Catholic, Patrick represents Saint Patrick, the Patron
Saint of Ireland. It may mean a lot to me; but to a Black mother about
to make a naming decision for her newborn – maybe not so much.

There is such a lack of accurate written history from Africa and
such a huge diversity of peoples in Africa that, it seems to me, a new
naming system may not be so out of line.

Law of Supply and Demand – Women in the Workplace

W atching I Love Lucy, Leave it to Beaver, or Donna Reed brings out the nostalgia bug. It sure seems that life was great in those days with mom at home to manage the house and kids, and dad off to work five days a week feeding a family on one paycheck. It seems like a family could be supported on one paycheck, even if it was from a laborer or a store clerk. What happened?

With a limited number of workers available, employers competed for workers and needed to pay a competitive wage to attract and keep the worker. Benefits and retirement plans kept workers on the job for a lifetime. It seemed like a good balance was struck.

In the 1960's as women began to enter the workforce in larger and larger numbers the law of supply and demand went into affect in the worst way for the working dads. Initially, clerical work went to women as did many lower skill jobs. Because there was a new abundance of workers available these became lower paying jobs and benefits were no longer as generous because the husbands had benefits from their job to cover wives and families.

As skill levels rose among women higher level jobs became filled by women and pay for the women remained lower than pay for men in equal positions. To make matters worse men's wages were relationally reduced, as were benefits, because if the man didn't want to work for the reduced offerings a woman would. As overall compensations were lowered it became impossible for most families to survive on one paycheck resulting in either the man working two jobs to maintain status quo or having to have the wife work a full time job just to maintain the life style that was affordable previously with one income.

Some of the major complaints today are that:

1. A single worker today finds it impossible to make ends meet by working one job,
2. Children are left with little parental supervision causing social problems which were less evident prior to the 1960's,
3. Benefits for workers are greatly reduced from what was considered fair in the past,
4. Pensions are becoming extinct requiring workers to take a portion of their salary for retirement which even further reduces the buying power of a paycheck, and
5. Workers no longer feel a loyalty to their job and so, are floating form job to job every few years instead of dedicating a lifetime to a career with one company.

This is a situation where there is no backing up Employers are enjoying low wages, reduced benefits and a supply of replacement workers to replace any disgruntled employees who are not happy with the compensation being offered.

Women have worked very hard to achieve their status. Families are the weakest that they have ever been in US history. Modern families have adjusted to living without the family summer vacations which seemed like such a common event for the Ricardos, the Cleavers, and the Stones. There should be no blame placed on women who simply wanted equality or maybe a nicer lifestyle for their families. The culprit was the law of supply and demand which allowed the marketplace to take advantage of the increased quantity of workers to crush families till half of all American families break up due to pressures of finance or increased job stresses coming from both parents instead of just dad.

It is less likely that dad can return home after work to the comfort of a waiting supper and a home managed by a full time mom. Mom now has not just job stress of her own but the additional pressures of trying to keep a home running, spending time with the children and a guilty conscience of not feeling like she is providing the mother figure that her grandmother did.

If anyone feels that this is off base please reconsider the facts without persecuting women for simply trying to improve their lot in life.

This, is the situation that we are in!

The reason that I feel that it is worth elaborating on is because I feel that we are on the cusp of the next part of the metamorphosis. Without having time to readjust, to try to salvage our families, and adapt to the current situation the next challenge is already on us and there will again be no backing up.

The next challenge to our financial security is the entry of millions of lower skilled workers who are reducing the earning power of our working class again. As the new abundance of workers makes American workers less in demand, how many jobs will it take a working class family to hold onto the lifestyle that we were attempting to adapt to? As more of jobs previously held by American workers are lost overseas to cheap labor and tax incentives the pickings are slimmer and slimmer for Americans. The claim that these are simply the jobs that Americans wouldn't do anyway is bullcrap. The reason that it appears that American workers won't do these jobs is because the law of supply and demand has reduced the wages and benefits for these jobs to a point that Americans can't afford to do these jobs.

Jobs in the industries which had provided a living wage for a hundred years can now be done by immigrants who are willing to live below the poverty line simply because it is better than the alternative back home.

How many Americans today live in homes that were bought and paid for by wages earned in mills or by clerks, policemen, or garbagemen? I personally know of many and so do you! Whatever you are being fed to make you believe that this is not true, don't believe it.

I don't need news reports to tell me what I need to believe. I've lived through the changes so far and am less than thrilled. I've heard life summed up by the best – "don't piss on my boot and tell me it's raining".

Left Handed Buyers

For a while it was popular to be left handed. Books were everywhere pointing out the benefits and drawbacks of being a southpaw. There is a market for left handed scissors, knives, and everything else that accented the uniqueness of lefties. It seems like the left handed slogan:' lefties are in their right mind' is chanted by every lefty on the planet. My saying is: with 13% of the world being left handed; when you do the math, that leaves 87% who wish they were.

Of all the lefty trivia books on the planet the one thing that I have never seen covered is what I consider the most unique feature of all; lefties buy their cars at the same time. It's been that way for years; for as long as I have been paying attention.

I work in a position where I see car buyers before they go home with their new car. For years I have been joking with lefties about the herd mentality of the lefty buyers. The reason I am writing this today is because I mentioned it to the first buyer this morning, who happened to be a lefty, and then the second, also a lefty. As I mentioned it to the third consecutive left handed buyer she thought I was kidding so I turned my computer screen around to show her that I had begun writing notes regarding this.

When in a lefty mode, most of the buyers are left handed with only an occasional righty. I'm not sure if that means that righties dry up or if all the lefties get a magic signal to buy a car.

This can sometimes go on for three or four consecutive days. Then they dry up. For the next month or more I may not see more than one or two lefties per week.

As I pieced these writings together throughout the day the next person was left handed and again I turned my screen around to show proof that I wasn't kidding.

Because it is not on a monthly basis, I can't even tie it to the moon.

Let Them Eat Oil

B ecause oil normally seems to come from countries that produce nothing else, it amazes me how those third world despots have gained the upper hand in the world. Countries that couldn't produce a transistor radio hold a strangle hold on the world powers.

Most of these third world nations have weak economies (in spite of billions of foreign dollars flowing in), weak national defenses, inadequate food production, and utterly corrupt governments. How did they get in the power position?

As we drain our treasury into theirs, aren't the options obvious? Let them eat oil! The stuff tastes like hell, even in the most refined forms.

Why does an alliance such as OPEC have to be the only alliance in the transaction? Without a market for their oil, most of the producers would be back in the stone age in a year.

It is only Western money and assistance that keeps these countries afloat. Most couldn't even refine their oil without foreign built refineries that are maintained by Westerners.

OPEC knows the importance of standing united to ensure the best money for their product. My goal would be to dissolve OPEC through alliances of our own for the purpose of oil procurement at a fairer price.

Knowing how fair minded and politically correct the world is today, OPEC has learned how to use this against us to exploit our weakness. There is no fear that a Western power would simply move in and take their oil so they use our good faith mentality to extort our economy.

This has turned into a one sided affair where they simply out think us.

This is so obvious to all that surely, our decision makers are being paid off to prevent retaliation. Corrupt decision makers must be selling out their own countries for personal gain because the desire for political correctness alone would not have allowed powerful nations to kneel before OPEC.

When it comes to leaders, why are we stuck with the corrupt ones who will sell out their loyalties rather than the aggressive ones like OPEC has? At least their guys are enriching their economies. Ours are draining ours.

Look For the Home in Florida

Watching the corporations fall like dominoes, the public is questioning why the bosses don't take hits. As the lower level investors and the employees lose their shirts, the CEOs still live large.

As an ordinary man I wonder if there is a common denominator? I seem to hear a bit of news every now and again about people taking advantage of the bankruptcy laws in Florida which protect the bankrupt from losing their homes.

The working stiff who suffers through the corporate mismanagement and loses everything through little fault of his own rarely has a paid out home in the state of Florida. It seems that quite a few of the mismanagers do however.

If a CEO, or anyone else in a command position happens to purchase a substantial home in Florida, would it mean that they are riding the edge of the envelope and are preparing to reduce the risk of failure? Even OJ has a house in Florida.

I wonder if the controllers of the lending institutions who have capitalized on the riskier loans and enjoyed the riches have protected themselves with Florida homes. What a racket, to have an untouchable nest egg after putting the screws to helpless victims. This couldn't have been the intent of the law.

Before investing in a company it may be helpful to know if the CEO has purchased a Florida home.

For the IRS or ethics committees to properly investigate improprieties I hope they also look for Florida home ownership. It may show intent.

May I Say, It Could Have Been Done If It Could Have Been Possible?

I love the nuances of the English language that are extremely intricate and are almost always taken for granted in everyday speech – except by English majors. How these are ever learned is a phenomenon.

I'm sure that most world languages possess many of these, but English has risen to be the accepted standard for some reason and I believe it's because you can express yourself more clearly in English than in any of its competitors.

An English professor spends a lifetime studying and conveying the idiosyncrasies of the language and has a name and definition for each word of each sentence of each paragraph. An ordinary person simply hopes to project a clear sentence without being embarrassed for his ignorance.

This 'to be' thing has got to be the most complex verb combination imaginable. 'Has been' is easy enough but it can also be a noun. How about 'had been' or 'had to have been', 'was to have been' and 'were to have been'; but no 'was to' or 'were to' *had* been.

'Is to have been' and 'will have been', but, again, not with '*had*'.

'Would have been' and 'could have been', 'had to have been' and 'must have been'. 'Not to have been' as opposed to 'will not have been' or 'would not have been.

What a language! Thank God for English majors.

This stuff with past, present, and future tenses is tough enough but the 'future perfect', 'past perfect', and then throw in the 'conditionals', is so complex that it seems that only a full time professional could handle it. A ten year old kid normally handles it quite well though, even before it is defined in the classroom.

Any kid can understand the difference between, something that, 'could have been done if it would have been possible' versus 'could have been done, were it possible' or can you say 'could have been done if it *could* have been possible'? How about: something that, would have been done if it would have been possible versus would have been done, were it possible' or 'would have been done had it been possible'. These may make good sense to a person but few people want to know why. The mechanics are simply robotic.

The complexities are never ending in English. "Can I go out?" "I don't know, *can* you go out?" "I'm sorry, *may* I go out?" "Yes, you may go out." This may be the daily routine between a child and a parent who studies English.

"Can I go out?" "Go ahead and drag your butt outside." This may be the conversation between a child and a parent who has never studied English. There's probably a happy medium in there somewhere.

A bit worse, may be 'I shall'. "May I go out?" may be a bit on the formal side but, "I shall go." is downright 'wimpish'! This goes to prove that there is a need for English teachers, but not as parents.

How about – 'should I go'? On the surface, it could be a straight question meaning, I'd like your opinion on whether or not I should go. To an English aficionado it would just as likely be the beginning of a sentence such as 'Should I go, I would expect adequate compensation'. What a language! The boundaries are never-ending!

If it *was* your decision . . . or, If it *were* your decision . . . The affect of the effect or is it the effect of the affect – how does one remember this stuff?

Media Words

Y ou gotta love the media when it comes to vocabulary. Present a new word and it becomes the word of the day for all media. The latest was 'vet' from 'vetted' or 'vetting'. Vetting is what it's called when you check someone out before giving them a position; especially for political appointees. It makes good sense when you hear it. I'm not sure how many times I had heard it used before this election but I've heard it many, many times recently. I don't think that it's even agreed on as to how it's spelled; I've seen it as 'vet' and 'vette'. The dictionaries refer to the word 'vetted' but then why isn't it okay to use 'to vet'? Maybe that's why it had had such limited usage.

The previous word was 'rhetoric'. For most of my life I hadn't heard that one in use very often. It's supposed to mean 'public speaking' or 'speech making' but it has become the politically correct way to say 'bull @%#'. Each politician or news pundit (another new one for me) calls the opponent's speech 'rhetoric' as a way to more politely insult him.

It's not polite to call someone a liar.

Prior to 'rhetoric', the word was 'demagogue'; another derogatory term. Where it used to mean a person who championed the causes of the people, it has come to mean someone who tells you what you want to hear, whether it's true or not, such as a politician filling the room with compliments and empty promises. I'm not sure how it went from a positive to a negative.

Why some words, such as these, catch on so fast among broadcasters is a mystery. I do know that when I hear an interesting one, I'm gonna hear an awful lot of it for the next few weeks. The words must come from the 'reporter's word of the day handbook'.

It used to be that way in management training jargon. In every course, and then in every subsequent conversation among the enlightened, words such as 'proactive', 'outside the box', 'synergy', or 'total quality' showed that one knew the secret handshake that separated the managers from the working stiffs.

One thing that you knew as you overheard the conversations where each person tried to impress the other with the use of the en vogue jargon – it was all rhetoric!

More to a GI Than Civilians Know

There's much more to a GI than most civilians could ever know. The ancient Spartans took it all the way into their culture. The honor of being a soldier was what all men aspired to. All aspects of the Spartan culture respected those who would lay down their lives for Sparta.

Our GIs are doing the deeds that no one else will do. They travel the world putting themselves in harm's way to keep those back home safe. Even though so many back home wouldn't give a rats ass in appreciation.

What makes a GI so special? Maybe it's the training. Far from the comforts of home, a GI gets to be abused for months to prepare to survive in his future endeavors. As an added challenge, part of this valuable time is now being dedicated to the humanities so that he can stay more politically correct as he risks his life in the performance of his duties.

The camaraderie that results from sharing the physical training and mental stress that only brothers in arms can experience forms bonds that last for a lifetime. The rest of society would envy the trust and friendship shared by our GIs if they could ever understand the power of it.

While the rest of American kids are bonding with their video games and enjoying the rush of make believe, our GIs are living it. To civilians – be jealous. It is a bond that most will never know.

Sometimes, while on a military base, I can still feel the difference. Recently, in a PX food court I watched my daughter walk by herself to make a purchase. I had no worries.

In a civilian mall I might be concerned for her safety but on post I would fear for the life of a potential molester.

The integrity of the GIs is far above that of the civilian populace. To be in the company of men who would lay down their lives to do the right thing is an honor.

Musicians Who Read and Musicians Who Don't

Nature produces two major categories of musicians: those who read music and those who don't. There's a need for each. Readers add the discipline and keep the classics alive. Until the 1950's most of the musicians were readers. They produced great music which could incorporate large orchestras and written music helped to keep the pieces organized. The musical education was normally formal and progression in the music world required the ability to read and write the music language. From Mozart through Glenn Miller, readers ruled.

Then along came rock and roll. From then on, most of the money makers played by ear: Paul McCartney, John Lennon, Jimmy Hendrix, Eric Clapton. Mostly guitar players; and most guitar players don't read music. Maybe because guitar doesn't lend itself to sheet music due to multiple positionings for the same note as well as nuances that are impossible to capture on paper.

Helping to add to the talent pool was the fact that most people could afford a guitar. And, guitars became sexy. Much more attractive on stage than a tuba.

With just a few simple chords, writer/performers like Neil Diamond and Hank Williams could knock out gold records. One guitar in the hands of a writer provided enough music to imagine the finished piece. Compare that to an oboe player. The guitar allowed the writer to sing as well as play and vocals were becoming more and more important in the rock and roll world. Although the Ventures were interesting, the Beatles dominated the music world.

The one common denominator among most of the popular musicians was the inability to read music. With non-readers dominating the music industry there was no longer a stigma to not reading, and no longer a need to donate huge portions of your time to learn the intricacies of written music. That time could be used in the creation of music.

The most creative people don't always lend themselves to the discipline and structure required to learn to read and write music. With only a minute segment of the population able to read music proficiently, there was a shortage of talent available from that community to provide music for the masses.

With so many new talented, creative members of the once exclusive music community, music was able to expand horizons and blues, jazz, heavy metal, soul, and country made music appealing to everyone. These formats are controlled by non-readers. Where does that leave the future for formal music education?

Mustard on Hot Dogs and Ketchup on Hamburgers

O ne idiosyncrasy of a true native New Yorker is: mustard on hot dogs and ketchup on hamburgers.

I never could take to the McDonalds formula of mustard, ketchup, pickles and onions on a hamburger. Throughout the world, the McDonald's empire grew and grew but never seemed to make way in New York City until they were able to offer special order hamburgers without an additional ten minute wait.

Special orders used to be the Achilles heel of McDonalds. Any deviation from the standard formula was called a grill order and it brought the line to a screeching halt. A piece of paper was passed to the grill and the wait began. Instead of simply leaving mustard off one of the cooking hamburgers, they would start a new batch for the grill order and cause a substantial delay in its delivery. This was contrary to what fast food was supposed to be, 'fast food'. This was also not very popular with New Yorkers, who are always in a hurry. This went on for years and probably cost McDonalds millions of dollars by not being able to adapt. One of their competitors finally said 'have it your way' and things changed.

For me there was one benefit of McDonalds' inability to adapt in those 'lost years'. During that time, I was an Air Force recruiter in New York State and my office was across the street from one of the busiest McDonalds in the state.

Knowing the 'grill order' situation, I would wait in the very busy line where a good potential candidate for the Air Force was cashiering.

When my turn came I would simply ask for a cheeseburger with only ketchup and ask him to please hurry. As the pressure rose I would simply mutter something about working for minimum wage and hand him my business card. Needless to say, at shift change, I could sometimes expect a visit from a disgruntled McDonald's employee.

Eventually, the manager would greet me at the door and provide me with coupons for free McDonald's meals. The stipulation was, they were useable anywhere, but there. He always knew when my coupons were gone because I'd be back in line, the longest line!

The metamorphosis of McDonalds into a true fast food restaurant, even for special orders, would have eventually dried up my source for new recruits.

Imagine, all of this because New Yorkers traditionally expected ketchup on hamburgers.

I don't think that McDonalds changed New York; I think that New York changed McDonalds.

My kids, today, put ketchup on hot dogs so I have considered paternity testing. They also dip French fries in honey mustard. What the hell is honey mustard? What's the matter with ketchup?

My Local Tire Shop

Just a note about the integrity of my local tire shop. I recently purchased two tires for my wife's car at COSTCO for $139.00 each, installed. As they were installed on the rear and the two best tires moved to the front, a noise appeared. Not sure it the noise was from the old tires, now on the front of the car, or maybe from a wheel bearing, I went to my local tire dealer hoping that they would be more capable of diagnosing the problem than the kids at COSTCO who simply install tires. I was prepared to pay a bit more for new front tires, if they were required, or the replacement of a wheel bearing if needed. The experience was educational.

The gentleman behind the counter was very helpful and took me to my car to educate me on the situation. He showed me how to rub my hand across the threads of the tire and verify that the solution was simple. The high spot and the low spot that he pointed out indicated that two new tires would make the noise go away.

There were no high and low spots on the tires! How many trusting customers have fallen for this scam? Some con artist convinces you that you can feel a problem that doesn't exist and you then trust him completely.

His estimate for the two tires, to match the two new tires that I had placed on the car two days at $278.00 was $705.00 and he guaranteed that the noise would disappear.

The one thing that I was sure of was that whatever he recommended was wrong. I went elsewhere and had the wheel bearing changed for $141.00 and the noise went away.

I wonder how many people he scams per day?

My Take on Arabs

I remember seeing a special on how a member of the Saudi royal family had taken the whole treasury on a couple of camels and wandered the desert to avoid losing it during the early part of the 20th century. It would take one hell of a camel today.

The Arabs have become the key players in the Muslim world today. Maybe because the Koran is in Arabic; maybe because they have a lot of money and know how to spread it around to accomplish their goals. With the Koran written in Arabic it ads a mysticism to the rest of the Islamic world by requiring good Muslims of all nations to learn Arabic to truly interpret the words of their prophet. The rational being that if the prophet chose Arabic then Arabic must be extraordinary. Arab money is the answer to the prayers of many Muslims throughout the third world. It supplies food and religious education, the two staples of third world Muslim life.

The Arabian Peninsula is a hot, dusty piece of wasteland where most decent farmland had been exhausted centuries ago. The people were nomadic dwellers who have offered nothing to civilization since the fifteenth century. It's a civilization which couldn't build a bicycle before the Western influx. Today, I wonder if they could produce a roll of Charmin. Think about it!

Then comes oil. Simply the luck of the draw. No skill involved, no ingenuity, no development. They couldn't even get it out of the ground without help. Half a century later they couldn't refine it without Western help. What a piece of luck! Raised their status quite a bit in the Muslim world. Maybe they convinced the rest of the Muslims that Allah put the oil in their control for a reason.

Unbeknownst to the most of the Western World, there has risen an aura of discrimination throughout the Muslim world. As Muslims travel the world it is very interesting to watch the interactions, or non-interactions, among Muslims. For example, a Saudi business man wouldn't let a person from Bangladesh touch his clothing. If you think I'm exaggerating just ask a Bengali or Afghan. The sacred preachings of Mohammad have no bearing on this hierarchy.

It makes me wonder how fast the Arabic world would crumble back to the dust of yesterday if oil became obsolete. Would the rest of the Islamic world come out from under the yoke of the Arabs if the Arabs no longer provided the money for the madrassas?

A number of years ago when the US was training military pilots for the Arabs it was comical to watch the rich Arabs kids react to the US way of life. With money meaning very little to these kids they would buy expensive American cars to use during their training periods and simply leave them in the airport parking lots when they returned home. The Islamic religious practices often disappeared while living in Texas. I guess it's as optional a religion as many others are except that they sure seem very devout as they cut the heads off captives or flog women for driving cars.

Before the power that was handed to these people, due to our need for their oil, it was much easier to maintain a peaceful coexistence.

Neptune

There used to be a seafood processing plant that used temp workers for the bulk of their grunge work. At the time, I worked for a temp agency as an engineering recruiter. Being the only man in the agency, I was responsible for some of the duties that the ladies were uncomfortable with.

There was a complaint from some of our temp laborers that they were being required to repackage expiring shrimp. I was sent to investigate and I learned quite a bit about the frozen seafood industry.

At the furthest end of the city stood the seafood plant. The plant was a poorly lit, fish smelling scene from a hundred years ago. Raincoated, showercapped workers were processing tons of fish of all varieties. The plant foreman was an Indian who looked like a slave driver from Gunga Din. He drove those minimum wage earners like they were in the slums of Calcutta.

The workers that I was concerned about stood at giant vats of liquid that looked like caldrons from Macbeth. The accusation was that they were being asked to open bags of frozen shrimp, defrost them and then refreeze them with a new freshness date.

As I looked around the plant it appeared very likely that this was true. There were hundreds of plastic bags of shrimp that had oriental writing on them which were being emptied into the vats of hot liquid and then refrozen and repackaged into plastic bags with American brand names on them and stamped with a new freshness date.

My temp worker had told me that the USDA inspector had restamped the new bags with the old shrimp so I spoke with him.

His response was that he was the inspector and that it was no one's business but his. His actions left consumers with shrimp that was up to twice as old as the date stamp on the packaging.

I did my report and let my company's owners take appropriate action. Today that plant is nothing but an empty building. I hope that the USDA inspector is not living off a government pension. It seems that you never find out the 'rest of the story'.

Most of America counts on federal agencies to be beyond reproach because they are responsible for our security and even the safety of the food we eat. As much as many of us would like government out of our lives, there is no safe option for these responsibilities because private industry is profit driven and cannot be depended upon to keep integrity ahead of earnings. When the most trustworthy agencies exhibit corrupt agents it is a lesson to 'trust but verify'. Very few people are 100% beyond reproach.

I have not had much experience with the commercial food world and I hope that the Neptune plant was the worst one in the country and that there are no more like it. I also hope that I ran into the only corrupt USDA agent in the country.

I do wish that my kids could have seen the working conditions of these temp workers. It would have been much easier to keep them motivated to study harder and never have to settle for such work.

New Homes for Gitmo'ers

There's a fanaticism by many liberals to provide justice for America's enemies. They profess a need for righteousness for Gitmo Bay detainees, even though these detainees desire to cut their throats. I've witnessed this on a local college campus and asked the demonstrators a question which cowered them to a person. My question was, "would you provide room and board for these people in your home until they can procure legal representation"? My concern is; how big is their commitment? Does it go beyond the excitement of demonstrating in the streets to expose the evil American Administration?

It appears that there is a limit to their bravery. They are brave enough to have these people released to kill other people's families but not necessarily their families.

Most surprising to me are the Jewish demonstrators. These Muslim fanatics would kill these Jews, to a man, simply for the fact that they are Jews. Tell me which is the most insane!

The funny thing is, it was Jesus who said to turn the other cheek. That's New Testament stuff. How come these Jews haven't become Christian if that's their true belief? That could rationalize their desire to forgive, and, remove a Muslim justification for wanting them dead. As a Christian, I may have just solved one of the world's greatest problems and gained brownie points for gaining converts. All Jews convert to Christianity.

For some reason, stories of detainees being released and being found back on the battlefield to kill again doesn't deter these idiots.

The latest finding is that the detainees should now be permitted representation by US attorneys. I guess that we will incur the cost. The saddest part will be the number of self serving attorneys who will sell out their country to grab a piece of the action while rationalizing that it is done in the name of justice. I can understand the motivation that these maggots have; money and recognition, but it's harder to comprehend the thought process of the protesters. It's probably that the hatred they have for the US is greater than their common sense.

New Yorkers will not Understand

Here's a scenario that is incomprehensible to anyone from New York City, Chicago, Boston, or Philly.

For people from the suburbs or smaller cities there is a strange phenomenon regarding cars. If you walk outside the boundaries of a mall everyone knows that you don't own a car. When you exit a mall and walk past the parking lot, it becomes obvious that you didn't drive.

You may be riding a bus, which isn't very cool outside of the big city.

In the big cities it is common to ride a bus or to take a taxi to shop. Elsewhere, it simply means that you don't have a car. If someone walks to the mall from their office, it is necessary to quickly get to the parking lot area because while walking through the vehicles, no one knows that you didn't just get out of your car.

When leaving the mall, there is a comfort level as you walk through the parking lot but it ends at the parking lot boundary.

In the cities, people walk to restaurants, theaters, and stores. The comfort level is fine because it's the norm. City people enjoy bustling sidewalks and the chance to escape the apartment. Outside the city it simply means that you need a better job to be able to afford a car.

Optimists vs. Pessimists

I once heard someone say that there is no such thing as gravity – the Earth just sucks. That surely shows the eternal pessimist.

To participate more wholly in the conversation, I like to interject that the glass may be half full but it's just that much more that's gonna spill when you knock it over. Leaning more toward the optimistic side of life, it is interesting to converse with the naysayers to maintain a more balanced life.

Although I'm sometimes accused of being too light hearted on some serious subjects, I try to take a more somber approach only on subjects with a hot button. Attacks on our military, first line defenders, national security, national pride, and family integrity and security are hot buttons. Almost everything else is up for grabs.

There are very few people who don't appreciate a positive attitude. Those who truly don't can kiss my butt anyway. Unfortunately, many of these maggots find themselves in customer service jobs or worse – supervisors of workers who are forced to toil under them for eight hours a day.

Nothing can be more frustrating than attempting to face the crab with a positive attitude and being shot down. It's kind of like the boot camp drill instructor who is prepared to wipe that smile off your face when there is not much recourse as a trainee. Fortunately, boot camp doesn't last forever but a bad boss can.

It's easy to say, "just quit that job and find something else" but for someone who has a family depending on a steady paycheck, it's not that easy.

On the other end of the spectrum, an eternal optimist can drive you nuts too. The excessive ones can lack the seriousness needed to do a job properly. They can fail to foresee potential problems, believing that problems won't arise.

Given the choice, I'd take the optimist because it's easier to add caution to an equation than to tolerate a maggot.

Our God is Better
Than Their God

An item which caught my attention and, I believe, reflects a cause for concern regarding American survival appeared on 60 Minutes. It was an interview with William Boykin, an army general. In a nutshell, this general is a true war hero, and leader, and Christian, who had committed the mortal sin of saying that our God is better than their god.

For this alleged infraction he had been reduced to bending and twisting his semantics to explain that this was not what he had actually said.

What kind of pressure could have caused this warrior to crawl on his knees and obviously back paddle on his true beliefs to stay politically correct.

If you believe it SAY IT! Our God IS better than their god! If their god is true and great then this is NOT the god that these maggots are affiliated with. Truly, Allah would not condone the actions of 9/11 and would never permit terrorists to capture a school, torturing and killing children.

Acknowledge the truth, if these terrorists could eliminate all of our children they would. They would use any means necessary, biological, chemical, or nuclear to destroy us and our children. They are affiliated with no God. Only what they perceive to be an excuse to attain their goals.

These vermin do not work under the guidance of a real Allah. They have contracted a make believe god who justifies their putrid existence and rationalizes a group of people who bring nothing to the table. Who have contributed NOTHING in hundreds and hundreds of years. Their survival depends solely on the success of the west. Without oil and the charity of the west to feed and employ their people, natural selection would erase them from the earth.

This huge section of the world which could not contrive a vaccine, design a refrigerator, or purify water without western assistance should show more appreciation for what our God has provided.

Scum who use their god to justify the subjugation of women and the maiming and killing of anyone who does not succumb to their interpretation of religious dogma do not deserve the precious attention of our political correctness police.

Say it General, "Our God *is* better than their god". It appears that you have had a great career and have commanded the respect of your troops. Don't sacrifice it all now! The people who are diminishing your self respect are the same people who are causing your troops to fight a civilized war against an uncivilized opponent who knows how to capitalize on this weakness. We haven't won yet because they know how to use our internal enemies. DON'T CAVE!

Paris in Our Backyard

A while ago my daughter requested a summer trip to Paris. Without even having to carefully examine the budget it was an easy response. No way!

I wasn't overly impressed with Paris on my one and only trip there many years ago. I didn't find it to be the cleanest city in Europe and it didn't seem to exude the magic that should be Paris.

As a compromise I suggested Quebec City which to me appears to be France in the eighteenth century. Although all of Quebec province is quite exotic, once you head east at Montreal it's a blast to the past. It is a bit of a drive but much better than eight hours in an airplane.

The 'Old City' is fantastic. It is full of life, and life there is still tied to the 17th and 18th centuries. The buildings are original and the pace of life is also. A tour is essential and very enjoyable. We were lucky enough to have an English speaking drive/tour guide who seemed old enough to have experienced most of the city's history. He also enlightened me to the fact that every Canadian official is a socialist and that every problem in Quebec today is directly attributed to socialism. This did not mean that he was in any way a fan of America though. The benefit of living in a socialist society is the attained ability to hate everything equally. Aside from his eccentricity, he was a wealth of knowledge on Quebec history and architecture. Little tidbits such as knowing the difference between original French of English buildings by whether the stones were natural or squared were extremely interesting. The life on the cobblestone streets, which have been continuously used for centuries, was electric. The melding of the ancient with the modern was like a walk through Colonial Williamsburg, supersized, and moved to France.

One of the most memorable items was the meal at Poulet Frit Kentucky, PFK, or KFC back home. The looks were the same, except for the PFK logo, which made the kids think that they were back home for a minute. When the mac and cheese was replaced with green macaroni salad and the French fries were served with gravy it let them know that they weren't in the US any longer.

All the ambience of modern day France and still just a day or two's drive. That did entice me to return to the 'Old City' and get back to the purpose of the trip, to enjoy France, pre-American Revolution.

I would recommend that trip for any family or history buff on a budget. It has the atmosphere of a city that only Disney could produce except it's the real thing.

Just a few hours west and you're back in the real world of the 21th century. Back to Montreal. Better than France. As modern as any city on the continent. Shopping that even two teenage girls consider great.

Pay Day Loans

Pay Day Loan or Title Loan businesses have opened in thousands of locations throughout much of the country. I don't normally see crowds outside their doors but they've got to be doing a hell of a business or there wouldn't be one on every block and one in each strip mall.

They are illegal in some states and some states are trying to shut them down or limit their interest rates but the sharks have been fighting back claiming that people have the right to utilize this service, if desired, and that the cost is actually lower than credit cards or some other more conventional lending sources. This would only be true if the figures are twisted beyond reality.

How they work is: money is borrowed from these sharks until payday. The amount is usually limited, by law, to a few hundred dollars and the period till repayment is usually one to four weeks. You simply write them a personal check to be deposited for repayment and they front you the cash.

For the Title Loans you assign your car title as collateral and take home your cash.

The amount of repayment is usually ten to fifteen bucks per one hundred borrowed plus an additional interest rate. Calculating the total of these, the APR is usually around *four hundred percent!*

I assume that because the loans are not at least a year in length they are able to skirt the annual percentage rate caps of each state. By keeping the 'annuals' out of the APR, it is not an APR.

It seems hard to believe that so many people could need a hundred bucks so badly that they would agree to such rates. And, if a hundred bucks is so detriment to their budget, how will they right their budget when the next paycheck ends up a hundred short? The profit is undoubtedly made by the consecutive rollovers of the borrowed amounts at the exorbitant interest rate.

It could be that people in this situation would not normally understand the rates anyway. It's kind of like the people who assess their car payment on a weekly basis instead of monthly. Many of these people would never accept a five hundred dollar per month car note although one hundred twenty five bucks a week is affordable.

Apparently there is quite a substantial underclass out there hiding beneath the radar of middle class America. If not, it would be a world void of Pay Day Loans, Title Loans, and Pawn Shops.

It seems that most of the states that prohibit this are in the north east. It's funny how certain subjects are sensitive to particular regions. Is it up to the government to protect these people from predators and themselves?

People Normally Agree

When I speak with people on a daily basis I find little disagreement. Most people believe in what I believe in. A strong military, the protection of our borders, rewards for working hard, and moderate taxes which are fair to all. Most believe that an American soldier's life is worth more than we have currently valued it at. Most believe that if a criminal breaks into your home and threatens your family's safety, that he should be willing to risk his life for that decision. Most believe that American jobs are every bit as important as corporate profit. Most believe that schools are not performing as well as they should for the money we are spending on them, and they know why.

Most believe that a 1950's family style is superior to the 21st century family style. Most believe that there is room for religion in our lives as long as it doesn't force itself on the lives of others.

It is rare that I find disagreement with any of these beliefs. Is it just the people that I congregate with? Do these beliefs make me a Democrat or a Republican?

Do I have to get down deeper in the subjects to find the party line?

Maybe it's in the next level down, such as the abortion subject. I do believe though, that if the staunchest 'pro-choicer' was forced to watch a partial birth abortion suck the life out of a kicking human baby, compromises would be reached.

If the subject was 'torture', the opinion would be the same if a family member's life hung on obtaining information from an unwilling perpetrator. Ideals are sometimes a luxury for ideal situations.

Would a 'Peta' member eat a chicken sandwich if it was all that was separating him from starvation? Ideals are commendable but underneath, Americans have more in common than is acknowledged.

The rest of the world has real problems, such as Muslim extremists killing little girls for attending schools; or African Muslims doing female castrations on their daughters. Chinese families facing sterilization for having more than one child, or Southern African men raping children in the belief that it will transfer their AIDS to the child; they are real problems.

American problems are so minor that political parties have to showcase our differences in order to win elections.

And on this too, most people agree with me!

Iraqi Christian Persecution

I hate to admit it but I watched 60 Minutes last night. The first segment was on the persecution of Christians on Iraq. The stories were horrifying. The suffering that these Christians endure to practice their faith is a wakeup call to all of us who take our faith for granted. This, it seemed to me, was not the point of their story. The evil of the murderous muslims was not the desired exposé of the reporter although any rational viewer should conclude this. The telling question he posed was in regard to the severity of the persecution before and after the removal of Sadam.

The question asked was, was the persecution worse before or after the US invasion? The answer given was, it is worse now that the Americans have disrupted Iraq. Sadam was a tolerant and liberal leader who even had Christians on his staff. What a great guy!

What was the desired result of this question posed to the Christian priest ministering to Iraqi Christians? To further the cause of the CBS policy to cripple the current administration. Their desire is to break the good will Americans have toward our military. It was not expounded how the radical muslims are the root of the evil, how the only reason it was quieter under Sadam was because Sadam needed the educated Christians and killed anyone who rocked his boat.

Although American soldiers were shown and interviewed, the piece was carefully crafted to downplay their role in restoring religious freedom and peace. Ironically, military transportation and protection was provided to the CBS crew so that they could safely stab the troops in the back.

How many people derive their opinions by watching CBS and trusting them to be objective and truthful? Millions! Having the freedom to poison the minds of trusting viewers sure seems like an abuse of the first amendment. How do you battle an internal enemy, such as CBS, who has the trust of so many sheep?

Post Election 2008

A s the very real possibility exists that conservative forms of communication, such as talk radio and free internet communication, may become restricted, it may become impossible to do anything but follow along.

The amazing thing to me was not just that we have lost our younger generation to the magic appeal of a gangster world where traditional values are history, but the electoral college was a slam dunk for Obama.

The popular vote was only 7% over for Obama. (not that the popular vote has any bearing at all)

We need to look into why the democratic machine owned the networks, the newspapers, AND the members of the electoral college which was alarmingly out of sync with the popular vote.

Remember, when Bush won on the electoral college, the popular vote was close, and so was the electoral college. Why was this electoral college a blow out????

Press 3 for Ebonics

I don't even know if ebonics is a word anymore but it describes a situation which is more easily understood just by the mention of the word. There is so much controversy regarding jobs being sent overseas and the rights of Black students to embrace their culture that I thought about the correlation.

I have always been a proponent of keeping American jobs in America. I have watched upstate New York wither on the vine as Hillary Clinton fans ignored the decimation that occurred on her watch. As the mills moved south of the border the economy collapsed. Houses in cities like Glens Falls are selling for the same price that they were bought for twenty five years ago. Taxes in the area are as high as they have ever been. Luxury homes and waterfront properties are still expensive because they are purchased by outsiders. The problem area is the affect on the real people. The people who were born and raised there, worked in the mills like their fathers had, and are now losing their homes due to unemployment. This is affecting whole towns as we speak.

For those who say that no one ever loses on real estate, let me mention a few words: Glens Falls, Detroit, St Louis, and soon to be California.

As the jobs leave America it is increasingly important to compete effectively for fewer and fewer jobs. A category of jobs that resulted from the computer age is customer service via telephone. As your computer, or entertainment system, or even cable TV requires service today, it is typically provided over the phone. Sometimes these tech help conversations have a substantial cost per minute. When a Black customer who has invested heavily in one of these systems has a need for assistance and is paying by the minute to have his problem addressed, will he prefer a conversation by an ebonics speaker or someone who is well spoken in English? If the customer has a choice to press 1 for English, 2 for Spanish, or 3 for Ebonics which will he choose? At a dollar per minute, loyalty to diversity, is out the window. When it comes to investing your money, you want the well spoken technician because there is an air of confidence that is inferred.

White customers certainly prefer the well spoken because when they have difficulty understanding the complicated instructions required to fix their high tech toys, there is no desire to have it become even more difficult by a language barrier and lack of confidence in the ability of the technician due to a perception of ignorance because of a dialect.

To ensure that this is not just a bigoted point of view I would love to see a press 1,2,or 3 option and see if anyone ever presses 3.

The threat to American jobs is real and serious and is increasing because of the desire for additional profit by corporations and lower prices by consumers. This is manifested by Wal-Mart, Kmart, Target, and a hundred more outlets for Chinese goods. This is also apparent by the huge number of corporations who have moved their customer service facilities overseas.

Customers are increasingly complaining about the language difficulties in dealing with foreigners and may make headway in returning these jobs to the US. The alternative must be better customer service, even if at a slightly higher cost. An inability to communicate with Americans will not help the situation. Learn English!

Professor Power

I just encountered a great money making opportunity. It works like a champ and is probably duplicated a thousand times each September and January. It is money made from a captive audience and is absolutely unchallenged as far as I can ascertain. It caught my attention to the tune of almost two hundred bucks.

An accountant professor at a Virginia university instructs from a book written by himself. The book is very expensive and I would expect that it must be a great book to command such a price. The book is a mandatory purchase and also a mandatory new purchase in that it is in its ninth edition.

What that means to a college kid is that there is no access to used versions of this book because assignments are derived from the current version only. To complete the assignments you must have the current version. When you have completed the course your book has no resale value because the next course by the same professor requires the next edition. Clever, monopolistic marketing!

If the book is worth this much money then why isn't it right yet? The subject is accounting 101 for God sakes! This is not a new subject and the concept does not change drastically each year. Where is the university oversight of this matter?

Progress Over Discrimination, Grandma

As bad as discrimination is today, I think about the stories of my Maternal Grandmother. As the story goes . . . After losing her husband who had fought for the British in WWI she was left alone in Ireland to raise two children. As most people know, that was not a very prosperous time nor place to live. Probably not unlike modern day Mexico. To provide the brightest future for herself and her children, she emigrated to England to raise enough money to qualify for a final destination of America. Every Irishman's dream since the famine.

As an added note, one of the most interesting parts of the story occurred earlier. In a letter home from the trenches, her first husband had requested a cigarette case. Her choice was between a lightweight tin case or a heavier steel case. She chose the lightweight case which was later pierced by a German bullet as he was shot through the heart. Try carrying the burden of that decision for the next 50 years. Funny thing about that decision; if she had chosen the other way and the bullet had been deflected; I wouldn't be here to write this.

After being approved to emigrate to America she sailed with two kids in hand to New York. In the pursuit of her dream she worked hard, remarried, and set basic education standards for her growing family. She eventually purchased a small apartment building in the Bronx which permitted her to take in boarders, normally young men who were arriving from Ireland in need of affordable housing with meals included.

The story continues that, being an Irish woman at a time when it was not beneficial to be Irish nor female in America, barricades began appearing. Although mortgaged to the max she was directed to install fire escapes on her building. When the fire escapes were installed she was informed that they were not installed as required by the inspector and must be redone. The cost being far beyond her capability; the inspector's goal was accomplished and the building was lost.

Her next attempt at the American dream was with the purchase of a bar and grill. A sure bet in an Irish neighborhood. To control losses from a husband who had more heart than business sense and who showed it by refusing to collect money from customers during the hard times, my grandmother spent much of her time managing the establishment. When one of her children was injured while playing, the innuendos spread that if his mother had spent less time in a bar and more time supervising her family, the accident would not have happened. Social pressure reduced her time managing the business and resulted in the loss of the business. Grandpa's big heart gave away more food and drink than he sold.

After her children were grown and gone there were other businesses started by this old Irish woman but she was clearly half a century too early to overcome discrimination.

Knowing my family history I do pay attention to the events of modern day immigration problems and the discrimination resulting from them. I understand the drive for people in less developed countries to make it to America. Being a realist though, I know the need for border controls. I know the need to ensure that immigrants lucky enough to be offered America's opportunities will appreciate the blessings of America and will contribute to America as Americans. My grandparents never returned to Ireland. They were Americans and raised their kids as Americans.

The other lesson I learned from my Grandmother's story is the potential of women in America and the losses to society as their opportunities are restricted by discrimination.

Who knows what great feats went unaccomplished during the past 300 years while we worked with only one half of our potential.

Rack n' Sack

R ack n' Sack – pick 'em up and put em' back. My kids still remember the mantra. As my kids were growing up, Sunday was our day together. Working two jobs didn't leave very much time so Sunday was always set aside to spend time together.

Depending on the budget, Sunday's activities were varied. One of the best was the Rack n' Sack – pick 'em up and put em' back.

Rack n' Sack was a local supermarket which was set up like a warehouse where you bagged your own groceries. Our Sunday outing to Rack n' Sack was rather unique. Each kid got his own cart and started at the entrance. The rule was: you could put any item that you wanted in the cart as long as it was non-refrigerated. Up and down the aisles the carts were filled with everything from chocolate donuts to junk cereal; anything that Mom wouldn't let you have. As we perused the stock the competition was to see who could have the most delicious cart full of treasures. By the time we reached the checkout the carts were filled to the top and both kids were looking suspiciously at the other's cart to get ideas for next Sunday's trip.

At the checkout counter the carts were turned around, back up and down the aisles, and each item was placed back in its proper place till the carts were empty. They had almost as much fun returning the goods to the shelves as they had had picking them up.

Any Sunday that Rack n' Sack was on the agenda was a favorite for the kids. As they got a little older it did lose its edge to the amusement park. For quite a while it did beat out a day at the beach though. No sand, no sunburn, and no one hour ride in the car.

Too bad kids have to grow up.

Radar in the Tunnel

2:00 AM on a Monday morning I was stopped at a road block as I exited the Chesapeake Bay Bridge Tunnel. As my turn came to speak with the officers I was told that I was traveling over the speed limit while in the tunnel. My speed was clocked by radar. I told the officer that his radar unit wouldn't function properly in that tunnel under those conditions and of course I was told to tell it to the judge.

Weeks later I told it to the judge. I brought along the specifications for the radar unit to show it's limitations inside a tunnel with other traffic present. My premise was that there was no way to prove the speed of a vehicle in a tunnel with other traffic present. Armed with this knowledge I felt no need for an attorney. Wrong!

After waiting for hours to present my case; those without an attorney go last in that Virginia Beach court, I approached the bench and was informed by the judge that, with 21 more cases to try before going home, she didn't have time for someone contesting a radar verified speeding violation. She didn't actually say, "without a lawyer". She did say, "guilty", though.

More ticked off than one man should ever be, I was asked to leave before being found in contempt. I appealed and appeared in circuit court a few months later.

Again, without a lawyer (I felt pretty strong about my facts) I appeared before a judge but this time there was a prosecutor also. I had overheads available, handouts, spec charts, and everything else that would fit in a briefcase.

I presented my case effectively enough that the prosecutor did not contest my info. The Judge found me not guilty and I was feeling that justice was weighted a little more evenly in the circuit court.

As I was gathering my paperwork the judge called the prosecutor to the bench and ripped his head off right in front of me. He asked him why he let a layman enter his court and claim expertise in his equipment. The prosecutor responded that the information was logical and he saw no way to contest it. I interjected that if my info was correct, and if a judge worked for both me and the prosecutor, wasn't his decision the correct decision? I was again threatened with contempt. It sure confirmed for me the value of having a lawyer. It's not whether you are guilty or innocent . . .

Regrets

O ne regret that I have is not having bought my mother a new car. No one that I have met ever deserved, or would have appreciated, one more. I've never met anyone who ever shared her possessions and time more generously. 'Mi Casa es Su Casa' was written with her in mind.

Talk about low standards when it comes to cars; she thought that a Ford Escort was a world class car.

For most of her later years the family transportation was in the form of a Plymouth Valiant bought from the phone company for a hundred bucks. These cars were olive drab (except for the rust), had over 100,000 miles and were three speed on the column. In the car world today this type of car is called a 'handshaker – no breeze', referring to the stick shift and no a/c.

Too bad she died so young; I could have really impressed her with a real car.

Retire, Train, Work

Just a thought on the sequence of life being backwards. The order of life after high school today goes: college (or training), then work, then retirement. My recommendation: retirement, then college (or training), then work.

Reason 1. How many kids are ready for college upon graduation from high school? None! The real desire is to see the world and 'find yourself'

Reason 2. How many college graduates are satisfied that they picked the right major and the right career field? None? Without experiencing the real world as an adult how can you know what you want to do for the rest of your life?

Reason 3. How many retired persons are truly happy to spend the rest of their lives in retirement, knowing that their usefulness and value to society has expired? None? Older workers appreciate the opportunity to be useful. They take more pride in their performance and usually find it hard to understand the complacency of the younger workers.

I propose that after high school, social security kicks in immediately. While in the prime of your life you travel the world, relax, find yourself, grow up. Start building a home if you please. Sleep till noon or live at the beach or ski slopes. Experience everything in life and decide on your future career at your leisure.

Depending on the career choice and the amount of college or training required, stage one ends between ages 35 and 40 and social security is repaid to the system as the worker works till age 80. All the time working with great memories of retirement and the knowledge that there was plenty of time to decide on an interesting career choice.

Think out of the box. Tell me I'm not on to something.

Roll Your Lawn

I was told a great story from a friend. While living in England he had a conversation with an English neighbor regarding the quality of the neighbor's lawn. He commented to the man that his lawn was superb and resembled the finest golf greens. The neighbor offered his secret. He recommended that he always buy the very best seed that could be afforded. He also recommended proper watering; the English being blessed with almost daily rainfall. Next, he recommended the purchase of a roller. This is a tool which is filled with water or sand to provide weight to a roller attached to a handle so that it can be rolled across the lawn. He guaranteed that if the roller was used once a month for 400 years, any lawn would look just like his.

This story always leads to further thought. One reflection is about our concept of time compared to European's. Probably not too many 400 year old lawns over here! To a European who has inherited family land for maybe 1000 years, there's a whole different concept of history. Most of our neighborhoods appear dated after thirty years.

To me it invokes the picture of the quintessential Englishmen I knew while living there. I had seen a care provided an English yard which I find rare in America. Without the opportunities for huge land tracts, such as are available here, every inch of property is prized and maintained by many English homeowners. Their yards are their contact with mother nature. There seems to be a special relationship with their minute piece of the earth. For normal Englishmen, without huge homes on huge properties the curb appeal is limited to the manicuring of that finite piece of property.

On one hand it reflects on what a great country we live in, and on the other hand, maybe our blessings are underappreciated.

Royalty

I never understood the concept of royalty. Living in England for a number of years reinforced my opposition to the concept. The argument with a bloke was always won when I asked why someone else's son is inherently superior to his. My kid may become president but your kid can never be king.

Royalty is novel and it's quaint but the notion is for the weak minded and insecure.

George Washington refused the offer, understanding that our system was the right one. Our democratic republic has proven superior to any other form of government for the past two hundred years. Royalty has produced nothing of significance but hemophiliacs.

The question today is: why the trend toward royalty in America? Why the lineage rights of the Bush's, the Clintons, and the Kennedy's?

In the 2008 Democratic presidential primary campaign it was assumed by millions that Hillary was the candidate. Post election, the talk is about Chelsea's political future. Out of nowhere, Caroline Kennedy became the heir apparent to the New York senate seat vacated by Hillary.

Even Donald Trump's kids are expected to inherit his empire. The adoring fans speak very highly and respectfully of the potential monarchs.

Our most popular leaders of the modern era: Reagan, Clinton, and Obama have come from plebian roots. All three would have been overlooked in a monarchy. The American monarchy advocates, in their desire to adore and to subordinate themselves to a greater being, overlook this fact.

Sabotage Prior to the 2008 Election

I would like to be the first to flat out accuse the machine of the left of sabotaging our nation.

The machine of the left includes not just democratic politicians, but newspapers and TV media who have invented, exaggerated, and distorted the economic problems of our country.

The purpose was to break consumer confidence to crush our economy and then to offer 'change'.

It succeeded far beyond their expectation and is still crumbling our foundation. The added benefit was the 'reported fall of Wall Street' and the 400+ page bill which contains provisions having nothing to do with its stated purpose. I believe that NO senator has read this bill! The 'pork' contained in this bill, which was to 'save our nation', should be written proof for the criminal trials which should be proceeding immediately. The problem is, these maggots will all be re-elected in November.

After **intentionally** crushing the American auto industry during these past weeks they are continuing to lie about the status of new car loan applications. Take it from some one who is 'where the rubber meets the road', car loans are available for all qualified buyers.

Their lies helped break confidence in the stock market which didn't need much help to fall with the inherent greed that already existed there.

My concern is that they will intentionally destroy the livelihood and retirement accounts of millions of Americans to achieve their goal of forcing a 'change' to their way of thinking.

They have almost half of the American public believing their lies. How much more damage can they inflict between now and November?

Segways

Touted to be to the car what the car was to the horse and buggy, I really was curious about what to expect from the new invention which was to be as impactful as the PC.

Back in 2001 the Segway was hyped beyond anything that I had seen in years. When released, it fell flat on its face. The Segway is a two wheeled vehicle that you stand on and travel up to 12 mph just by leaning in the direction that you want to go. It's electric and quiet. Good, economical transportation!

I tried one; it was great! What wasn't foreseen though was that the world hates them. In most areas of the world you can't use them in the street because they are too slow for traffic, and you can't use them on the sidewalk because they are too fast for pedestrians.

To keep them off the road, municipalities around the world have provided restrictions which have made them impossible for public use.

They are currently limited to the streets of Disneyland and a few bicycle paths around the world. Even on my ride through Fisherman's Wharf in San Francisco the police interrupted the tour to restrict its use.

Where was the research prior to its release back in 2001? How could people who helped develop such an advanced method of transportation have been so blind? In retrospect its limitations seem so obvious. Where do you park them? How does a city dweller get them up the stairs to their apartment, or up to their office? What happens when it rains or snows? With a range of roughly ten miles, what about suburbanites? Where was the market research?

At this time it appears that the only solution would be the construction of bicycle paths throughout the world. Too bad; they really are neat.

Senate Priorities

Heard the 'news on the hour' a few minutes ago and it again confirmed that the US Senate is still pandering to whatever liberal bastards are keeping them in position.

The Midwest is drowning under the latest floods and there have been more deaths reported. Our food supply is being threatened by grain being redirected as questionable fuel additives and tomatoes poisoning more people with salmonella. Our domestic fuel production isn't making a dent on our true needs and OPEC, along with crooked, unscrupulous speculators are draining the dwindling funds of the average American household. Production of trucks and sport utilities are crushed. The dollar is at a level so low that even the Chinese imports are becoming too expensive. The Pentagon reports that China may be hacking into top secret data which will affect national defense. With all this going on, the Senate will investigate to find out who gave permission to torture a terrorist.

Their first hint – look for the man who has yet to be emasculated. Try to find the last politician who will risk his career and freedom to protect the citizens of this country. If you find him; before you embellish your career with his blood, thank him for keeping your family safe. Thank him for keeping my family safe, for if it was up to you, you would have my guns confiscated and I would have little chance to protect my family when you neuter the protectors of this country.

Why does it seem so clear to me that we are being manipulated into feminizing America and that while our enemies watch us lose our desire to defend ourselves we will become the class sissy who gets his ass kicked even by the smaller kids because that's what bullies do. The problem is, we can't call on mommy because there is no mommy to save us.

SST

A number of years ago while still in the employ of the United States Air Force I created a program which I titled SST, an acronym for Suggestion Solicitation Team. I pitched it to Richard Meyers, who later became Chairman of the Joint Chiefs of Staff, in a private meeting at Langley Air Force Base and he put his blessing on it.

My intent was to solicit suggestions from military personnel to make improvements for the Air Force. The Air Force had a suggestion program which had very little positive impact on improvements and offered very little incentive for anyone to participate. I felt that it was simply an excuse to employ civil service workers and provided very little benefit to the Air Force or Air Force personnel.

My first experience with the Air Force Suggestion Program was with an idea I had had to save money on an aircraft modification. I had proposed a modification which had a cost of two or three dollars each and could be handled locally and immediately. Months later it was turned down because a similar modification was already being accomplished for thousands of dollars each; and at another location, which was requiring the aircraft to be out of service for the duration of the modification procedure.

Upon studying the suggestion program that was in place I decided to propose an alternative program. The current program offered very little incentives to submitters and produced poor results. It made submitting suggestions labor intensive and made it much easier for suggestion evaluators to turn down the suggestion rather than approve it. Most of the program administrators spent their time hyping the few successes that they had.

I formed a team to solicit suggestions at the ground level, remove the burden from the submitter, carry a good suggestion all the way through to approval while making continuous improvements to the suggestion, and rewarding the submitter quickly and proportionately to encourage more suggestions.

What I pitched to Meyers was a team of people at each base, made up of specialists from various fields to travel to the worksites with laptops to solicit ideas from the troops, brain storm the idea, and carry the idea through the approval process to the evaluators who could not disapprove the idea. The evaluating expert was required to apply his expertise to tweak the suggestion until it became a money maker. Previously, the evaluators customarily found excuses to disapprove a suggestion to get it off their desk quicker. My team took the burden off the evaluator by assisting in the research, documentation, and implementation.

The teams were to be made up of personnel who were not actively mission essential due to injury, obsolescence, over manning, or whatever made them available. I wanted the guys who were on crutches, in casts, or on light duty excuses for a hurt back. I was the perfect candidate because my particular aircraft type was terminated and I was awaiting retirement with not enough time remaining for a reassignment.

I was given quite a team to work with and ended up as a dumping ground for personnel but still managed to save millions of dollars on just the one base. My time was spent advertising the SST at commander's calls and at the worksites directly, and chasing down new ideas for submittals.

It was quite the challenge developing new software, fine tuning the new program, managing the members, who sometimes outranked me, and fending off the base air Force Suggestion Program personnel who obviously considered my program as a threat to their existence. To make it worse, all suggestions worked through my program were required to be submitted through and credited to the base Air Force Suggestion Program.

One of the most difficult parts was that the concept was so new and exciting that team members alone were submitting more suggestions than we could handle.

By eliminating the option to turn down a suggestion during evaluation, great things happened.

One interesting suggestion regarded the nomex flight suits which were needed for the new area of operation which was the desert terrain of the Mid-East. The flight suits were green but the terrain was brown leaving a downed pilot easily visible to the enemy. A suggestion was submitted but was immediately turned down because it had been submitted previously through the Air Force Suggestion Program and turned down due to cost constraints.

For my team, this was an unacceptable reason and the investigation began. Upon correspondence with the nomex company it was revealed that the nomex fabric was manufactured in brown and was being dyed green, at an extra cost, to meet Air Force requirements.

The possibilities for savings and improvements were endless. We worked every type of improvement imaginable. We went directly to the technicians who were performing maintenance on anything from bombs to aircraft and asked for better maintenance methods which could help us to rewrite the technical orders for better efficiency and cost savings. We solicited ideas for aircraft parts which could be locally manufactured at a lower cost while still meeting military specs.

With each suggestion the goal was to pay a percentage of the savings to the suggestor and do it within thirty days, as opposed to the half a year or so that the Air Force Suggestion Program was averaging.

I had submitted the Suggestion Solicitation Team concept as a suggestion through the Air Force Suggestion Program to avoid a conflict of interest and was awarded $75.00. I did, however, receive a letter form Vice President Al Gore, after I retired, to inform me that my idea was being considered for incorporation in his 'reinventing government' program.

That was the last that I had ever heard about my program.

When I retired there was no longer anyone who was willing to battle the personnel of the Air Force Suggestion Program who had been accepting full credit for my team's success to ensure their survivability. Hopefully, the competition helped to improve the Air Force Suggestion Program.

Stares

I wonder if there is a college course on stares. If there is, it probably puts confusing names to stuff that everyone already inherently knows, just like most other liberal arts college courses.

Stares are probably worth a college course. The subject is as valid as human sexuality, ethnic studies, sociology, or psychology. Stares are just as fascinating.

If you stand in a crowded room and someone from across the room is staring at you, you can feel it. Even though you don't necessarily even see them, you can tell when you're being stared at.

If an out of towner rides a New York City subway and inadvertently stares at someone, it can be the cause of an incident. Americans don't appreciate being stared at, especially New Yorkers. In some countries it is not unusual for people to look at each other but it is simply not done here. A New York response to a harmless stare can be 'whach u lookin at?'.

Stares do make most people uncomfortable. A person who has put on a couple of unsightly pounds feels sure that everyone else is noticing and any glance is considered a stare. Conversely, any one who has shed a few pounds or is sporting some new clothes is looking for a stare for an ego boost.

One can possess a lot of power through a stare. Seeing someone who may have lost a few pounds or maybe has a new hairstyle, a short stare with a slight smile can make their day. It can change their whole mood from apprehensive to confident. Just with a stare!

A stare at an attractive woman can have a myriad of results which can almost justify a whole other college course for this subject.

Witnessed by your mate, it can cause serious injury. Witnessed by the recipient of the stare, it can make both of you feel uncomfortable.

Even though young ladies may dress provocatively to attract stares they can sometimes appear insulted if they are stared at. Witnessed by her boyfriend or husband, a stare might also get you killed.

I would guess that the same woman would also feel disappointed if she was completely ignored after trying so hard to attract stares. That one probably belongs in one of those other college courses like human sexuality or psychology.

Stateside Fatalities

Watching the local news tonight the first report to give me grave concern was a young Virginia Marine who was killed by an IED in Iraq. I still can't fathom the idea of why American kids are worth less than Iraqis; why our future is allowed to die horrible, painful deaths while we still have bombs at our disposal. This is a disgusting waste of American lives. If we have no leaders with enough guts to take on the media than we should just give it up and accept the status of a loser. Until the enemy believes that our kids are worth more than their kids and that we would not choose to enter a war lightly, but will eliminate all traces of any threat to the US, we will be losing young, valiant, irreplaceable, American lives.

The next report was equally as important. Another shooting occurred last night. In the Hampton Roads region of Virginia, as in so many other regions of America, a person is killed virtually every night. If it's not a drive-by then it's a break-in or a convenience store robbery gone wrong. I believe that we are killing more of our own people than Iraq and Afghanistan combined.

Children are killed by being shot through the walls of their houses by stray bullets. Lowlife animal scum are entering banks or stores and killing clerks for the sake of recreation. Many are caught on camera and the predatory maggots show no remorse.

It seems like these scumbags should be the ones traveling the streets of Iraq attracting sniper fire and IEDs instead of the heroes that are voluntarily offering life and limb for what they believe to be a noble cause.

Both of these news stories report a tragic waste. Both are reducible if sane leadership prevailed. How does someone ever decide which is worse?

Strange Car in the Neighborhood

W hile walking the dog this morning I saw a strange car in the neighborhood. Driving past me was an older Mazda 626 with a rear window broken out. From what I could see the driver was a darker skinned female with two young men as passengers.

What is the proper reaction? In my area of Virginia, Hampton Roads, there is a shooting two to three times a week and violent break-in of homes and businesses on a regular basis. The newspapers report that the perpetrators are almost always young Black men. White crime is normally the perverted high school teacher who is caught soliciting students.

Seeing a car with Black males that do not live in my neighborhood presents a dilemma; if I investigate it the appearance is that I am being prejudice by assuming the worst; if I don't, and there is a problem that I may have prevented, I would be a very poor neighbor.

My question is: whose fault is this? Is it bigoted to profile in a situation such as this or is it insane not to?

What if the young men in the car were White? With the overwhelming number of violent crimes in Hampton Roads being committed by non-whites, should one report the out of place vehicle to the police anyway, simply to remain non-prejudicial?

If the dark skinned passengers of the vehicle were from India, what should be the reaction? I have never seen a violent crime reported about Indian kids in Hampton Roads. Is this also profiling?

If the car had three Mexicans in it, what would be the most likely reaction? In my area there is low crime rate by Mexicans so a safe assumption is that the vehicle would be delivering laborers for yard work or home repairs. There is virtually no Latino gang banger activity here in that most Mexicans are fresh from Mexico and are simply here to work and avoid drawing attention to their situation as illegals.

These are all prejudicial assumptions based on the observations of local crime rates.

Whose fault is it that these questions even exist? If most violent crime in South-East Virginia involving shootings, break-ins, and burglaries are committed by young Black males isn't it prudent to be skeptical in an unfamiliar situation?

In a Black neighborhood would a group of Indian kids pose a threat to the inhabitants? Would a group of Oriental kids cause discomfort? Would a couple of White kids be likely to cause trouble while stopping in a convenience store late at night? Would a couple of White kids be likely to find trouble while stopping in a convenience store late at night?

Would the situations change if everyone would assume that there should be no profiling for any reason? If everyone would put their newspapers away maybe there would be new hope for the elimination of bigotry.

In spite of all the social injustices, is there a chance that if the perpetrators of violent crime would cease and desist, that all strangers to a neighborhood could be viewed equally?

Suicidal Jews

As a gentile, I find it difficult to understand the mind set of many Jews. Possessing a heritage and religion that is so enduring and strong, what makes so many Jews so rebellious? I would think that a legacy so steeped in traditional conservative values would foster conservative ideals.

Instead, many Jews appear almost suicidal in their political views. The roadblock to the survival of Israel does not seem to be coming from the Muslims alone. American Jews appear to provide most of the obstacles to the protection of Israel. From Jewish politicians, to Jews in the entertainment field, to Jews in the business, academic, and scientific world, opinions seem, often, to be liberal and anti-Israeli. This is simply an observation by an ordinary gentile with no dog in this fight.

Modern history has seen an extraordinary Jewish influence on revolution, anarchy, and extremist causes in general, in the United States and around the world.

During the Russian Revolution, although the Jewish population in the Russian region was a minority, many key players in the Bolshevik Party, including Leon Trotsky, were Jewish. With a party doctrine to eliminate religion, what fostered their drive to destroy the forte of Judaism, the Jewish religion?

Karl Marx, the father of communism, and also a Jew, considered religion to be the opiate of the masses and did as much to damage Judaism as anyone since the Spanish Inquisition.

Why is it that Jews so often become zealots of liberalism and anarchism? From the antiwar movements in the US in the 1960's to the antiwar movement today, some of the strongest supporters are

Jewish. Being such a small minority of the American population, they are disproportionately represented in the media, politics, and private concerns as anti-establishment, anti-Israel, and antiwar. Possibly the largest financial contributor to the extreme left movement in the US, George Soros, is also Jewish.

Something appears to draw many Jews to extreme causes. The writings of Emma Goldman and Alexander Berkman perpetuated the public's apprehension of Jews in the early 1900's making many in the public believe that most Jews were anarchists. During the Bolshevik Revolution, the contribution of American Jews to the Bolshevik cause increased the uneasiness. Common belief among American Christians in the twentieth century was that most Jews were communists, especially in New York and later, Hollywood. When I was a kid in New York City, many of the adults believed that the majority of New York City school teachers who were Jewish, were communists. Upon reading biographies of New York Jews, it appears that this wasn't far from the truth. Today, with the stigma of communism waning, it is talked about more openly.

Now that communism is no longer en vogue as a rebellious cause, activist Jews seem to gravitate to new causes. One of today's causes is globalization.

Many gentiles believe that Jewish concerns in the US lean toward a relaxation of borders and a subordination of American power to a world control. This is the speculation of the Republican Party toward the Democratic Party where the overwhelming majority of Jewish politicians reside. The Democratic Party is also where the liberal agendas regarding 'Global Warming', 'environmentalism', 'gay rights', and 'free choice', dwell.

I have always been curious as to why so many famous Jews become atheists. From Karl Marx, to Sigmund Freud, to Carl Reiner, to Michael Newdow, who sued to have 'under God' removed from the Pledge of Allegiance.

It certainly is perplexing to a gentile, why so many Jews appear to be so out of synch with a religion that, to the untrained eye, should be conservative in nature and loyal to the survival of the State of Israel.

Sunday Morning TV Religion

O ne of the smoothest religious scams that I have ever witnessed occurred on a Sunday morning religious broadcast. On that particular Sunday morning I woke to the TV having been left on from the previous night.

Attempting to sleep in, I tried to ignore the TV. It soon caught my attention as I heard a man apologizing to the viewers for his indiscretion. With all the degenerates and crooks that slip into the religious world I had to hear more.

He explained that his daughter had recently given up her mission to South America and that that had put pressure on him BUT, that was no excuse; he would take full responsibility.

Pressures from within the ministry had pulled his full attention from the mission, but that too was no excuse for his lapse in judgment. He was prepared to stand before God and the world and accept full responsibility. Even the illness of a close relative was no excuse for his lack of adherence to his Christian obligations.

By this time I was wide awake because I had to see the face of this penance seeking sinner. I was curious as to whether his congregation could ever forgive his sin. I was curious as to what this egregious sin had been. Was he trying to come clean before the National Enquirer outed him? Or, was the sin so severe that his conscience could no longer take the stress.

As the show was coming to an end, he still hadn't revealed nature of the sin. This man could sure set the scene for a climax. Maybe he was trying to hold off the painful truth so as not to have to endure the agony of questions from the congregation.

With scant minutes left of the broadcast he finally came clean. He fought back tears and begged forgiveness as he explained that while standing in his study he was drawn to a beam of sunlight shining on the page of his Bible. He exclaimed that his Bible sat on its stand and the light from the heavens lit up a passage that read, 'If you don't give, you won't receive', and he knew at that instant that he had deprived his followers the passage to heaven.

He had remembered that he had neglected to request contributions during his last broadcast and his listeners would not receive salvation because they had not given.

He apologized profusely and hoped to make it up to them by offering to accept contributions from them for which he would send them a gold trimmed Bible, similar to his own, for four hundred dollars. If the four hundred dollars was not available you could still find salvation by making installments to the ministry and a Bible would be coming your way.

I had never seen this preacher before but I knew that he was magic.

If it had happened today I would have saved it on my DVR and googled everything about this shyster.

How many older widows had fallen for this maggot's line and now sport a four hundred dollar Bible with the assurance that they now have their passage paid in full?

Surgeons Cut

A bit of common knowledge in the medical community is that surgeons cut. In and of itself, not a revelation. However, armed with that knowledge, a layman may make completely different decisions when obtaining medical care.

Ask a mechanic if your car needs a tune-up and what do you think the response will be? He doesn't get paid if he says no. Ask a surgeon a similar question and what do you think the answer will often be? Take a problem to a general practitioner, be it a wart, a mole, or a questionable adenoid or tonsil, and the GP will consider freezing a wart, biopsying a mole, and running tests or antibiotics for adenoids or tonsils.

Take the same problem to a surgeon and what would be the treatment? Surgeons cut!

GPs normally don't have the financial incentive to perform surgery and are limited by license to minor procedures. Their normal practice is normally to treat through non-surgical means when possible. A surgeon's practice is narrower in scope and forces a limitation on their knowledge of alternative methods. And, the big bucks are made in the operating room.

Who could blame a surgeon from wanting to practice his craft?

To Sign or Not to Sign

T he question that exists regarding the back of a credit or debit
card is, do I sign or not?

For mine, I choose not to sign. My reasons are, that I choose to
have my ID checked when my card is used. And, if my card is stolen,
my signature is not available to the thief. It may prove that it was not
me who used the card.

The cards often say that the card is not valid if not signed.
Once signed, any thief has the last piece of the puzzle and so the
quagmire.

I have yet to have a card not be accepted without my signature
except for the US Post Office. This is standard policy at the Post Office
and each time that I encountered it, there was no exception allowed.
My explanation was not appreciated. Without another method of
payment, no service was permitted. I was not allowed to provide
additional proof of ID with signature verification.

The method of using an unsigned card is to sign it in pencil to
complete the transaction and then erase the signature. It's worked for
me. Government workers %#^*!

Taking On My Own Church on Contraception

If there is one subject that I disagree with the Roman Catholic Church on, it is contraception. The biggest threats to health, wealth, and happiness throughout the world are overpopulation and disease. It is a matter of basic survival in much of the world. It is also the cause for immense suffering and misery in locations like Africa where draught and famine are rampant.

A proclamation from the Pope will never stop sex from being performed and Rome has never provided enough aid to feed the numbers of children produced there. Neither has it supplied the medications needed to treat the spread of AIDS which could be reduced by the use of condoms.

It appears that Rome is fostering and encouraging procreation into misery, suffering, and certain premature death. It is also promoting the spread of sexually transmitted diseases in an attempt to adhere to a doctrine which Jesus had never directly commented on[4]. In cultures where men will sodomize children to attempt to rid themselves of AIDS, the Pope should be funding condom distribution centers. The Christian thing to do would be to ease suffering, prevent unwanted

---

[4]   Precedence is normally attributed to Onan of Genesis fame but his true crime may have been the breaking of Jewish law by not fathering a dead brother's child for selfish purposes. This was also a time when the need for survival of the race was procreation. Today it is just the opposite.

births, and attempt to make right the problems caused because this was not done sooner.

Even in the US the Roman doctrine causes misery. Catholic couples who adhere to the Church's dogma are continuously under pressure to abstain or overpopulate.

The result has been for millions of Catholics to back away from the Church. Rome's interference into the most basic functions of humanity has been a dismal failure. Normal Catholic couples do not respect an illogical edict from someone who has never had a normal sexual relationship and has not produced adequate proof that this is truly the desire of God.

It seems similar to the Christian sects who permit their children to die rather than allow the interference of a doctor. Religion is misinterpreted and the results are forced on the followers; and rarely to their benefit.

If the Catholic Church was dependent on a congregation that believed in and adhered to this statute, the Church would dissolve in a generation. I suspect that most priests who live in the real world and witness the damage done by lack birth control and disease prevention are at odds with Rome.

The zealots are always the ones far removed from the effects of bad policy.

The Beatles Had Two Tracks

I always try to keep abreast of the advances in the music recording industry. For me the easiest way to do this is by reading musical instrument catalogs. Even though I don't have any affiliation with music today, other than listening to music while walking my dog, I'm always tempted to look into the new digital recording decks just in case I want to become a star.

The fascination is with the capabilities of musicians today to record, at low cost, in a bedroom, with greater recording power than was available to the Beatles while they were cranking out million seller classics in the best studios available on the planet. So where are the new classics?

Recording with only two tracks and very little room for mistakes, the greatest music of the modern era, and the most covered songs, were cranked out simply by the genius of the writers, performers, and engineers/producers. Lennon, McCartney, and George Martin in a studio could put together, in one afternoon, a hit which would be covered 100 times and impress people even today for the brilliance of their synergy.

If given the availability of today's equipment, could this be duplicated again? Could they have produced even greater music? Or, would their time be lost on the equipment instead of the music?

They seemed to handle the incorporation of orchestras, synthesizers, and multi-tracking okay. Buddy Holly seemed to handle his access to string sections well and even pioneered new uses for classic instruments while still cranking out the hits. Why has it all but disappeared?

With great quality recording equipment available to almost anyone today, where are all the hits? Where are the Lennon-McCartney quality hits? Isn't there a kid sitting in his bedroom preparing to save his genius on disk for the rest of the world to enjoy?

Maybe one reason is the video game revolution which has taken the kid who would have been spending his time, drive, and ambition with a guitar or piano to channel his creativity into something for posterity, but today prefers the drug-like rush of his Wii.

This video game infusion sure is costing our culture more than anyone will ever know.

The tools are available today to gain access to the genius which is sitting in the head of some musical prodigy; and to allow him to produce even greater quality works than ever before. Mozart could hear only one instrument at a time while writing and needed to compile a whole orchestra to hear a finished product. What could he have done with a synthesizer and a 24 track studio in his room?

The Colonel Bumps the Girl

A number of years ago I had an experience that had a major influence on how I directed the rest of my career. As a young airman in the Air Force I usually made extra money by playing in a local band during my time off. On night while playing on stage at the officer's club I had a revelation which I still reflect on. As I remember it, the head table was just below the stage which put me within earshot.

In those days bumping was all the rage on the dance floor and a colonel who appeared to be the commander of the head table group was taking advantage of his rank and dancing with the young officers' wives.

Not all the wives enjoyed bumping with the colonel and one lieutenant's wife was fairly offended by the old groper. Being on stage and so close to them I got to experience the whole drama. Each time he was lewd with the lieutenant's wife she would tell her husband that she wanted to leave and that he should do something about the situation. His response was different than mine would have been. He said to her that she should be patient because he could not be the first to leave. In consolation, he would take her home at the first opportunity.

It's quite easy to offer suggestions as to how one should properly handle such a situation, however, I believe that that lieutenant knew the writing on the wall for that situation. Not much chance of a win with that one. His path of least damage, he decided, was with his wife.

A thousand times since, I replayed that scene and could see that under the same circumstances my career would have ended at that very moment. I would have never been able to forget it if I had not taken any action.

In retrospect, it would be easy to say that I would have simply kicked the crap out of that old pervert but, thank God, I wasn't required to make that decision.

That experience has remained an influence in many career decisions throughout my life and has probably cost me more money than I should have allowed it to.

Who knows if it's an old hippy mentality of not selling out to the establishment or a John Wayne mentality of machismo overriding evil. Either way, it can make one gun-shy of entering a situation which could ever lead to a compromise of integrity.

The Drug That Is Video Games

The videogame is one of greatest technological advances in the history of the world. It can put kid in the middle of a medieval battle with lifelike dragons and other assorted monsters. A kid can play tennis and feel the thrill of the game and never even get off the couch except to replenish his snacks. He can play guitar like a real guitar player and never even have to learn how to tune a guitar. It can offer all the thrills of racing a car through the Indy 500 track or even through outer space using a lifelike steering wheel and controls.

Kids, and adults, will sit for hours, upon hours, upon hours in front of a video screen and never even come up for air. The same people who cannot sit in a classroom for 45 minutes at a time without a drug assist because of an attention deficit disorder.

The video game also doubles as a babysitter and can keep a player in another room so that you don't have to compete for the channel changer.

The amazing graphics and sound can place you in a drug like state which can isolate you from reality and transport the player into a world of fantasy in which you can kill and be killed time after time. It completely eliminates the need for human to human interaction. No more need for kids to play cowboys and Indians, no need for tag, no need for football, baseball, or hockey. There's no longer a need to learn how to play a musical instrument. Someone else has already done the programming and you can just make believe that you are talented. One can now be entertained forever. What a life!

What is the cost of all this high tech entertainment? The equipment is normally a few hundred bucks with a few hundred more invested to keep up with the newest advances. The games themselves are normally only 50 bucks or so and each game can provide hours of entertainment. For the kids whose parents don't automatically provide them with the latest games, some may even work a few hours a week to feed the addiction.

What else does it cost? It costs the same as crack! It costs the loss of real life ambition from our kids. It costs the time that might have been spent conversing as a family. It costs the time that may have been spent studying, in the past, but now takes every spare minute of the student's life. It costs the health of our kids today who are either too fat or too thin because they no longer go out to play with their friends. They either sit in front of the screen with a bag of chips or don't eat at all because meals just steal time from the game. It costs the loss of access to the potential brilliance of a kid's mind because so many kids are not studying musical instruments anymore because you can now play make believe guitar hero without ever knowing a thing about music. It may be costing us the next Paul Simon, or Beethoven, or Pavarotti.

What's the difference between video games and drugs?

Thank goodness that John Lennon only turned to drugs. What would we have to show for his legacy if he had turned to video games?

The Importance of a Car

The car means different things to different people. This is based on US car owners. In most parts of the world owning a car is so far beyond the grasp of reality that it will never be a player in their lives for the next five generations.

I would prefer to say that I am way too practical to ever worry about color, style, or bells and whistles, but I had purchased a vehicle in southern Virginia without air conditioning or even power windows and ended up keeping it for 17 miserable summers of driving. That won't happen again if I can help it.

Vehicles are definitely reflective of buyers and are often distinctive to gender, culture, and race. For example, first vehicle choice for most people from India is Toyota. Camry, if you are successful; Corolla, if you're still working on it. Good, basic, reliable cars and never any add-ons beyond what the factory offers.

Chevys and Fords for the all-Americans. Dad and grandpa owned them and tradition means a lot. It's rationalized by sayings such as: "they're getting better, having to compete with the imports."

Black buyers will buy the big Sport Utilities if possible. The Escalades and Navigators; and decked out! Aftermarket rims and the works. If that is not possible; then the imports. Japanese name brands hold status, and, provide dependability which is very important. A vehicle can hold a larger portion of the budget than is normally acceptable to an Oriental buyer. A young black buyer had told me once that, "they don't have to see where you live but everyone knows what you drive."

Oriental buyers are often distinguished by being either first or second generation. First generation citizens are normally extremely practical in their decision. A Honda Civic or a Nissan Sentra with automatic and air. Period! No frills, no thrills. Interest rate matters as much as the vehicle. The numbers on the contract override the enjoyment of the vehicle. Many have told me that it is part of the American dream but not as big a part as owning a business to provide for future generations.

Second and third generation Oriental buyers are completely the opposite. Acura instead of Honda; unless it's a tricked out Civic si, like in the magazines. Ground effects and spoiler! Sometimes the parents are making purchase for the kid and although completely contrary to what the parents would recommend, it sometimes seems like a badge of success to have placed their offspring in a position to be able to make such a flagrant purchase.

American females are usually very color conscious of the exterior and if there are kids involved, the interior. They often have the forethought to anticipate the spilled Coke and are more selective on these then the men in their lives. Women are also more appreciative of customer service during and after the purchase of their vehicle and often will choose a Saturn even if their men try to convince them that it is nothing more than a Chevrolet with plastic sides.

Realtors buy larger vehicles to accommodate buyers. Expensive, large vehicles if they require an air of success to impress their customers or inexpensive large vehicles if they desire to express a more pragmatic image.

If you think that I am off base on any of these stereotypes just look out your window at the next traffic light. Ask anyone who has been successfully selling vehicles for a while or ask a car insurance salesman.

The Musical Hook

I love the hook. From Beethoven's 5th with the big dum dum dum dummm . . . To Chuck Berry's intro to Johnny B Goode playing off that big 'A' barre. That hook has been the hook that let the early rockers know that Chuck Berry ruled the guitar world. The snappy 'Proud Mary' intro filled the dance floor for 25 years. That sexy B3 Hammond intro to 'Whiter Shade of Pale' made many a couple dim the lights.

The Doobie Brothers were masters. The minor feeling guitar lick from the intro to 'Long Train Runnin', or 'China Grove' pounding out the power 'E Major' chord; these guys were brilliant.

Pete Townshend's 'Pinball Wizard' slamming that 'Dsus4' – 'D' was strong enough to build a rock opera.

The intro to 'Tush' could make you picture ZZ Top commanding a Texas stage and that great bassline into 'Badge' still makes every 'power trio' fan from the sixties wonder where real music has gone.

For the more mainstreamers, Kool and the Gang's 'Celebration' had that fantastic intro which was a guarantee to get any party going. Everybody loves a great hook.

John Fogarty seemed to put a strong hook in every one of his songs and remember, CCR had more double sided hits than any band in history. That's how to effectively sell your hook talent.

There doesn't appear to be that magic today, no great hooks such as that guitar beauty from 'My Girl'. Many of the rap artists are actually buying the rights to classic hooks to sample into their songs to add credibility to their meager attempts at music. Why don't they just write their own hooks and leave the classics alone?

The Newest Tax Increase

The latest mantra is 'no tax increases'. There will be more 'stuff' for everyone though. How can it work when there's no money and no new money coming in from tax increases? The solution is more tax money. How?

The Republicans say that money will trickle down from the lower taxes on the rich. Bull! The rich simply get richer as we have experienced by the millionaires and billionaires who are taking bonuses in the millions after crushing their companies and expecting government dollars to support their losses.

The Democrats say," increase taxes as long as you increase more on the rich".

As long as there are two parties, neither is an easy solution.

The answer is to increase taxes without the knowledge of the people. The way to do it is to print money in specific amounts.

Because money is not backed by gold, or anything really, it is a great tool for an enterprising politician.

It works like this: decide how much tax increase you need to support your desires, then print the appropriate amount of dollars.

The proportion of newly printed, non-backed bills to the amount of the current treasury balance is the tax increase. For example, printing one trillion dollars will devalue the money in my wallet by the percentage of yesterday's overall treasury value to today's new, perceived value. Here's the trick. Yesterday's treasury value and today's are the same because there is no additional gold, or anything else, to increase its value so . . . your dollar is worth that much less and thus, a tax increase without a tax increase. It simply takes more of your money to make your purchases.

Your retirement savings have been devalued. Your bank account has been devalued. Your social security check is worth that much less. Therefore, you have to work that much longer or harder to get back to where you were yesterday.

What's the difference between that and a tax increase where they take your money through increased taxes, and your having to work longer or harder to get back to where you were before the tax increase.

The difference is: because nobody told you, you didn't realize it.

The Nuts on the Block

G rowing up in New York City in the 50's and 60's was probably the best experience that anyone could have. As kids there, we had more fun than any kid in the world should be allowed to have. We had great experiences and great friendships that have endured all these years.

On the occasions that we are able to get together these days to reminisce, the one subject that fascinates me is the amount of nuts that existed on just one small city block. Out of just the five buildings on my block we had enough nuts for a whole city.

At the time, it was comical to experience life with the nuts. Today I should be more socially sensitive and forget the unfortunates but it sure makes for great nostalgic conversation.

In the corner building there was a woman who hated the noise from the kids. With most of the kids living two to three to four or more to a bedroom, life existed on the street. All spare time was spent on the street. There were no video games or computers. We were limited to real sports and real games, thank God. Needless to say, the streets were loud and she hated noise. Her remedy was to throw Clorox out of her window on the kids who dared to play underneath. This was not very popular with the girls who were obviously worried about their hair and clothes. Clothes were in short supply for a kid who sometimes had no more than one or two drawers to store their whole wardrobe.

To aggravate the poor woman even more, the boys would sometimes squirt lighter fluid on their desert boots, knock on her door in the dark hallway and run down the hall, when she answered, with their shoes on fire. No wonder she was nuts.

In the same building was another woman who would occasionally go off her meds and throw items from her fifth story window. The items would be anything she could get her hands on including frying pans, pots, and anything else that could fit through the window. Fortunately, her windows were in a courtyard which kept most of the items from reaching the pedestrians on Broadway. When she was off her meds everyone knew it.

My building had the most nuts and with my father being the superintendent of the building, I was privy to every occurrence. There was a man on the ground floor who would sometimes jump out of his window. Sometimes it was the front window which was only a few feet off the ground but sometimes it was the rear window which was over ten feet off the ground onto concrete. Every time he would start, his wife would call my father for help. The problem was that this man was exceptionally strong when he would go off. One time I saw four cops and two civilians attempt to subdue him and he threw them around like dolls. My poor father, although a very strong man, had a hell of a time with this guy.

When he moved out of that apartment, the next tenant was just as nuts. This woman was paranoid and when she lost it she would run from her apartment wearing whatever she happened to have on. Sometimes, nothing at all. She spent quite a few nights at Bellevue. When she was normal, she was the nicest person on the block so she had quite a few visitors at the hospital. Seeing her on the ward left quite an impression.

Right next door to that apartment lived an old woman who kept cats; lots and lots of cats. Her apartment was so full of junk and cats that you couldn't see the floor except where she kept a narrow path clear.

She traveled occasionally to a slaughterhouse where she purchased beef blood which she enjoyed quite a bit. For her age, she appeared quite healthy so maybe there was something to it.

She owned a nice little home hundreds of miles away in upstate New York and sometimes managed to procure a ride there with a number of her cats during the summer; she, like most people on the block, didn't have a car.

Down the hall from her was a nice guy who hated kids making noise on the fire escape outside his bedroom window. Some of the poor shift workers had a tough time living on a block full of kids.

One of the games that we kids played was throwing a basketball through the rungs of the ladders of the fire escapes because there were no basketball hoops on the block. Not knowing when he was trying to sleep, we would sometimes wake him up and he would come out the window like a madman and chase us around the block. Thank God that, even in his rage, he was not a very fast runner and he never caught anyone; but I remember a number of times crawling under parked cars to stay out of his reach till he gave up and went home. The next time you would see him he was perfectly normal.

Upstairs in my building lived a retired cop who had a great story. The story goes that he had the Time Square beat for most of his career and that one day his superiors discovered that for all those years he had never given out a single parking ticket. When they realized the loss in revenue that he had cost the city he was forced to retire.

He opened up the corner bar each morning and closed it up each night. His one trip off the bar stool each day was to stumble home singing 'The bells are ringing for me and my gal'. He slept only until the bar reopened in the morning. He was sure as clockwork.

Two buildings down there was a tragic story. A kid had had his face massacred during an altercation. The stitching was terrible and in an attempt to get the work redone he joined the Navy hoping that his medical benefits would pay for cosmetic surgery. When he was informed that elective surgery would not be permitted he hung himself on his ship.

As if there weren't enough nuts living on that one block, there was also a nut who wore a collar and pretended to be a priest or a brother and spent his money on the guys hoping for some repayment. He would take a few at a time in his car to Lake George or any place that they wanted to go and try to convince the guys that he was a man of the cloth. They let him hang around till his money was gone. I never heard what had happened to him although there was a bit of speculation that he hit a homerun with some guys from another block.

With all the nuts on one small block, we were mostly oblivious to it. It was just part of life and it makes a much larger impression today in retrospect than it ever did then.

The Oil Situation

Just one man's opinion of the oil situation. The recommended solution seems to be to increase gas mileage, reduce driving and home heating usage to reduce consumption. My opinion is that lower consumption simply means that the supply of 'unfriendlies' oil will last longer and prices will rise to maintain constant profit.

To reduce the burden on the American consumer and reduce the flow of American dollars to unfriendly suppliers there are some other options which are not publicly offered:

1. *DRASTICALLY* reduce consumption to the point that oil production from domestic and friendly sources will suffice. This would require homes to truly be efficient with oil priced 'through the roof' for waste and greatly reduced for the conservative. Vehicles can't settle for 20 or so percent better mileage. It's gotta be 300+ percent so that it won't be just the Japanese perfecting hybrids and alternative fuels vehicles. If a' manhattan project' could develop an atomic weapon sixty years ago, it can develop a proper battery today given the right incentives. With government so deeply in our lives already, maybe this would be the one acceptable cooperation between government and U.S. industry.

2. *TAKE THE OIL.* The U.S. has already paid a huge price for mid east oil. Popularity throughout the world is not our forte anyway. If it is not desirable to reduce our consumption then areas such as Iraq, Venezuela, and Mexico owe us and debts should be collected.

3. *ALTERNATIVE OPEC.* Currently, if we don't buy OPEC oil, the rest of the world will, because they have to. By developing, and patenting alternative energy sources, vehicles, and power production we could be the suppliers to the world. As the U.S. developed nuclear energy in the 1950's the rest of the world benefited and in some cases, bypassed us. An additional benefit is that the 'unfriendlies' who hold power simply because of oil supplies will be disempowered. OPEC members seem to show the greatest animosity towards us anyway.

In my opinion, any of the three options are better than our current situation. It would be great, however, to see the U.S. back in the position we deserve.

The Villages of New York City

There were great advantages to growing up when and where I did. The village life was great. The small town feel where everyone knew their neighbors and everyone shared common beliefs, had a common background, and often, a common future was magic. Most were of the same heritage and the same religion. You knew everyone and rarely encountered strangers. The kids went to the same schools and church.

All parents were respected and all parents looked after all kids. Kids were safe at all times in the village. Sports were played in the village with close knit teams who competed against nearby village teams in friendly rivalries.

All kids, young and older were safe to play on the streets, even at night because all kids were protected by all other villagers.

Activity was nonstop on the streets and shopping was nearby and patronized by the village residents. It was a great village life which kindled friendships which have lasted more than half a century. One hundred yards away was the next village and another hundred yards away was the next, and on and on and on.

My village was 213th street in Manhattan. It was mostly an Irish Catholic village. It was one block long with five apartment buildings on one side of the street and a telephone company building on the other. That made it one of the smaller villages but that didn't appear so apparent because it was teeming with life.

Each apartment building averaged forty to fifty families and being overwhelmingly Irish, there were kids; lots of kids; kids of all ages. Each kid knew every other kid and every other kid's parents.

Most families lived in a one, two, or three bedroom apartment with up to ten kids in a family. There was no room for privacy so your life was spent interacting with everyone else in the village. Kids slept two, three, or sometimes more to a room and the parents often slept on the castro convertible in the living room.

Meals were normally eaten as a family in the kitchen. I don't remember seeing many dining rooms.

Clothes were limited because space was limited in the apartments. When your assigned drawers were full and your' under the bed' area was full, you were done. To add a new pair of shoes, an old pair must leave. A new shirt meant that an old shirt must go. There were few extras. A spare kitchen drawer could hold dad's tools; a hammer, pliers, screwdriver, and some spare nails in case a picture was to be hung. No need for lawn mowers, weed whackers, rakes, shovels, power saws, drills or anything else that appears in most of the village homes outside of New York City. They were rarely needed. There were few projects in the homes. Painting was normally done by contractors sent by the superintendent of the individual building at the agreed upon year sequence. Without HGTV there was little incentive for home improvement projects. By today's standards it would appear that every apartment looked just like the rest but to the trained eye each was as unique as any home in America today.

Without large, private homes, yards, gardens, garages, sheds, and pools; without pool tables, big screen TVs, or computers; without dens, rec rooms, studies, or exercise equipment; without clothes dryers, freezers or even air conditioners, it didn't take much money to live. Recreation and entertainment were provided for, and by, each other.

Most moms stayed home to raise the kids. They made sure that the kids got to school and to church and that the homes were as respectable as possible. Your apartment was called your home or your house. It was what you knew and provided all that you expected. As far as anyone knew, this was how the civilized world lived. As a matter of fact, most considered this a privileged life and considered any one living anywhere else lacking.

Every need was satisfied in the security of the village. It was never called a village but in retrospect, it should have been.

All the necessary socials skills were learned in the village. There were very few secrets in the village. Very little diversity in the village, although it appeared that there was.

No outsiders entered the village unnoticed so the people were always safe. Ten o'clock on a summer night could find kids still playing touch football or stickball on the street and a toddler on the street was always under the protective eye of all other villagers.

Kidnappings, murders, muggings, rapes, and violent crime of any type was virtually unheard of.

Being mostly Irish, it was assumed that most would aspire to become cops or firemen or union workers to follow in the footsteps of the Irish from the previous generation. Almost all voters were Democrats and Catholic. I can still recall meeting my first Protestant. I had met very few kids who did not attend the same Catholic school as I did. We all had the same teachers and even went to the same school dances as each other. I met a girl who lived nearby and knew that she did not attend my school. When she told me that it was because she was a Lutheran, I was fascinated. She looked quite a bit like the normal girls.

The first progression from the village for many of the kids was due to high school. High school forced associations with kids from neighboring villages who attended the same grade school as you. High school for Catholic kids meant bus and subway rides across New York City to far flung areas far from the safety of the village or even the neighboring villages so associations were essential.

The village life made great impressions on the lives of thousands and thousands of New York City kids and has formed bonds that have lasted decades and decades. To kids of wealth from the suburbs and towns across America it may appear that the New York City kids lacked the material goods possessed by the rest, but they were rarely missed and I don't know of many who would have traded places with anyone else. The friendships and camaraderie proved more valuable and enduring than any material items. The most talked about regret by most New Yorkers is that the villages are gone. The peace and security enjoyed by us is not available for our children so it was necessary to join the rest of America and settle for second best for our kids; the house in the suburbs, the pool, the two car garage and the regret that all of that could never substitute for the real thing.

Things My Kids Better Never Have Done

Things that I considered normal and fun as a kid growing up in New York City, I would kill my kids for today. Being a typical suburbanite today, I have always taught my kids to stay out of the street and on the sidewalks. This, in retrospect, sounds a bit hypocritical from someone who played most sports in traffic. Stickball, kickball, touch football and skullzies were played while sharing the street with cars and taxi cabs. I don't remember anyone ever getting hit by a car. Maybe the kids were sharper or the New York drivers were more considerate.

My kids were taught to sterilize everything that they touch. My friends and I passed around soda bottles among everyone who needed a sip. Runny noses or sneezes excluded no one. I don't remember any more illnesses then than I see now. Maybe exposure to every germ known to man built up a stronger immune system.

In the basement of my building were dumbwaiters where carts on a rope and pulley system ran along an unlit vertical shaft from the basement to the apartments in the five stories above to collect garbage from the tenants. Many times we would take turns riding in the garbage cart up the five story shaft to have a way to amuse ourselves. Everyone survived. My kids were trained to never touch the inside of our trash can. Lysol keeps them safe.

My kids know to be careful in the pool in our housing development and to avoid the kiddie pool because some of the toddlers do not wear the correct diapers for swimming. We swam in the Harlem River and swam like hell when the sewers emptied into it to avoid the unsavory contents of a New York City cesspool. The brown water normally cleared up after a few minutes and back in we went.

It feels really healthy to watch kids in my housing area play tag in their back yards. The fences protect them from running near the cars and most yards have a playground with swings and slides that look like wooden forts. We played tag on the streets, in the basements of the tenements and on the roofs of the buildings five and six stories up. They were the greatest games of tag in the world. I never lost a single friend to any serious injury.

At the end of my neighborhood was a city bus graveyard where old buses were parked till they were disposed of. Maybe a hundred of them were parked tightly together and it provided one of the greatest playgrounds that you could imagine. You could hang out inside the buses or climb onto the top of them and play tag while jumping from one to the next. It was more fun than any playground and had so many places for a kid to hide that we could play for hours and never get bored. I hope that my kids can enjoy similar experiences with video games.

I remember a great story about those buses. Before the buses were taken away for crushing, I had decided to take some of the reflectors to use on bicycles, or home made scooters. To pry these reflectors off the buses I borrowed a screw driver from my father's shadowboard on his workbench. Being the superintendent of our building, he had the only tools that I had ever really seen. He was very particular with his tools and each one had a place and every tool was in its place.

That particular day, the cops arrived at the bus yard as I had a fist full of reflectors and my father's screwdriver. Needless to say, everything was confiscated before the cops let me go. My only concern was the screwdriver. I had no way to replace it and my father would kill me if he found out that I had touched his tools, never mind stealing the reflectors. I never said a word about the event; never, not even till he passed away forty years later. The odd part was that a screwdriver appeared on the shadowboard a few days later. I never found out if the cops knew my father because he worked near the bus yard and they were all city workers or if he assumed that he had lost it and replaced it with another. That will remain one of the mysteries of my life.

Think You're a Libertarian?

A popular claim today is to be Libertarian. Maybe because some of the Conservative radio talk show hosts claim to be. The concept is that a Libertarian wants government out of our lives and to strictly adhere to the Constitution. If it's not in the Constitution, it has no business in our lives.

Given enough money, a lot of money, this is an idea which could almost work. However, welcome to the real world. The Social Security Administration is nowhere to be found in the Constitution. Remove Social Security from the equation today and there would be millions of elderly Americans completely destitute. Many people work a lifetime barely getting by and have no pension plans available. What would happen if there was absolutely no money when old age prevented gainful employment? When the population was much smaller and life expectancies were much lower, family and the Church were the social security system. Compare that to a population of 300 million with more and more people living nearly 100 years.

As bad as public schools are today, picture the country without them. The middle class might disappear completely. Even for the worst of students, the government schools at least provide eight hours of child supervision to allow the parent to work. There is no provision in the Constitution for government schools.

There are also no provisions for road works or the interstate highway system. If it were up to private companies to provide these services every mile of road would have a toll on it to compensate for the construction and maintenance. Countries are only as great as their road system. If goods cannot get to market the economy cannot survive. There are no great nations without great roads.

Different states have different degrees of social services available to their citizenry. New York is considered a very liberal state and is one of the states that attracts huge numbers of immigrants, both legal and illegal. The tax payers in New York pay huge amounts of taxes to support the social programs but are better protected from catastrophes than many other states.

Years ago, while still a New York resident, I had accumulated huge medical bills due to a sick child. At almost $1000 per night for the intensive care unit alone, my federal insurance bailed out leaving me with hundreds and hundreds of thousands of dollars of personal liability. If I had been a resident of almost any other state, the results could have been ruinous. At that moment I was personally glad that I had been a tax paying New Yorker.

It's easy to claim the Libertarian cause when you haven't appreciated the benefits of government programs. I wonder how many libertarians are on the government 'no call' list for their home telephones?

As conservative as I am regarding the security of America and protecting our culture, I know that we have the most perfect balance of Conservatism and Liberalism on the planet.

Basic nature causes people to tend to choose one side of an issue or the other and to lend zealous support to that chosen side. With the cheerleaders from the extreme right and the extreme left competing for our souls the overall balance has been surprisingly amazing.

Thoughts 3/31/2007

My reaction to headlines about Brits captured by Iran.

Just a thought concerning the reaction of the British sailors and marines in Iranian custody.

My first thought was regarding how fast they turned on their mission and country. My second thought was, WHY?

Initially I thought that maybe they were pre-briefed that, if captured, respond to interrogation with whatever keeps you alive till you are rescued but on second thought, the truth may be that they know they will never be rescued. The press has already destroyed the hearts and minds of the British military just as they are trying to do to ours.

Reading everyday in their own press how evil England and the US are and knowing that every soldier, sailor, and marine is expendable, how much faith could they have to believe that they will be rescued? Every newspaper reading warrior is aware that their countrymen no longer believe in the mission. Their countrymen no longer believe Britain is GREAT.

Their countryman no longer believe that freedom and security are worth the cost.

The captured have no reason to believe that they will ever be rescued. Their fate lies in the hands of Iran – NOT Britain.

The warriors have been stripped of the belief in God and Country. Their mission is not noble.

Compound this with the pressure they are undergoing as prisoners of muslims who have already cut the heads off previous prisoners.

These muslim maggots can show western reports to prove that the mission is worthless and lost.

How could a prisoner of war maintain faith?

We are next! We are allowing the enemies among us to chip away at our beliefs. To erode the belief that the safety and security of America is worth ANY cost.

The majority of the news media, most of the politicians, and most of the entertainment industry have jumped aboard the self-satisfying bandwagon to destroy our will to protect our American way of life. Their mission is to destroy OUR military's will to fight.

Would we rescue our troops?

Thoughts 10/21/08

My thoughts during the 2008 campaign.

How come McCain doesn't use the words 'welfare state'? The promise by Obama *is* a welfare state with the verbiage carefully chosen so as not to awaken the ire of the real American workers. Say the words John!

The most adamant Obama supporters are the least likely to be negatively affected by the welfare state.

Will Hollywood and the news media be affected by the welfare state? Probably not. Major Hollywood players don't touch money on a day to day basis. They have agents and managers who make sure that they are provided for. It's easy to be generous when you don't feel it directly in your wallet. It's sort of like the difference between having our taxes taken out on a weekly basis rather than the government mailing a bill for all due taxes on April 15th. That would cause a revolt. Ignorance is bliss.

The news media generally run in packs and the most aggressive Democrats there live on expense accounts with their own money well protected from having to be donated to the impending welfare state. Remember the reports of Clinton money being safely tucked away in the Cayman Islands while squawking for us to share more with the unfortunates?

It's easy to be generous with everyone else's money. To me, it's similar to the person who wants the borders open, but keeps locks on the doors to his home.

Where did all the ACORN workers work before the campaign? How do they expect to eat after the election is over? Can all these ACORNERS who are currently registering Democrats to vote for Obama and driving them to the polls really expect to be fed when their jobs disappear? Yes! They do expect to be fed! It does explain their dedication to the cause.

Thoughts 11/15/2008

I have had the opinion that the bulk of our economic problems have been purposely fabricated to damage our economy. The purpose may have been to influence our election and/or for the personal gain of some power players. I thought that it was beyond coincidence that the crush of Wall Street came a month before the election and not the day after, or three years prior, or any other less opportunistic time.

They offered 'change' and it became 'all about the economy'.

I did not base my accusation strictly on the fact that George Soros had already done similar damage to England in 1992 and that this time many of his associates have profited immensely and have furthered their agendas not by aiding our economy, but by sabotaging it.

In looking for assurance that I was not simply feeding paranoia I looked to my local region. In the Tidewater area of Virginia the local economy is also in a slump. Retail sales are down and reports of a bleak Christmas selling season are similar to the rest of the nation.

A major segment of Tidewater has had no impact from a down turned economy. It is largely a military population with Norfolk Naval, Langley Air Force Base, Fort Eustis, and quite a few other bases. The largest single employer beyond the government is Northrop Grumman shipyard which employs 19,000 people.

Virtually none of these workers have had any loss of income but still our retail industry is tanking just like everywhere else. Why?

The media has convinced people who are immune to job losses, pay cuts, and health benefit concerns that their lives now suck. In fact, we are now paying almost half of the price that we paid just a couple

233

of months ago for gas and local people are still afraid to purchase new vehicles.

After having controlled a US Presidential election and still fighting to provide a 'super majority' to secure complete control of the government, who can provide resistance to these people who have won the hearts and minds of the uninformed?

Thoughts English POWs 4/7/07

I wrote this in response to the news coverage of British military personnel who were captured and immediately proceeded to embarrass themselves by selling out to their captors. No resistance was exhibited but they returned home to a hero's welcome.

I wonder how emboldened the muslims are now that they see the actual resolve of the British. The reports by the ex-captives say they were placed in stone cells in isolation and made to sleep on rags. They even heard guns clicking.

For this they sold out their integrity and their country.

Maybe the problem is that these were English marines and sailors. Normally the real work was done by Hessians, Irish, Scottish, and Gurkhas. Where was that stiff upper lip? The story is compounded by the hero's welcome they received back in England.

I'm sure that the fear factor in Iran and the rest of the muslim world is safely on zero at this point.

Is there any question as to how the 'manly' standards are set so low and how hard we try to live down to them.

As it becomes increasingly unpopular to be masculine in the western world we sometimes forget that the rest of the world isn't keeping up with our unisex, 'feel good about ourselves' renaissance. Thank God we have bombs! Wait! We're not using bombs. They are! We're fighting the civilized war and will punish any soldier or marine who doesn't play by the rules.

The British have achieved this plateau of the totally civilized fighting force. We're working on it.

Timing

I was always fascinated with creative musical timing. The first that stood out was "Take Five" by the Dave Brubeck Quartet back in 1959. It had that great feel which came, partly, from that 5/4 time signature. I wouldn't want to try to dance to it. The old box step might require you to have one extra leg.

The unusual time signatures are very rare in popular music and I don't know of too many before John Lennon recorded "All You Need is Love" as a Beatles smash. That song should be a train wreck but it was a world wide hit. George Martin must have thought that it was time to adjust Lennon's meds. Who writes in 7/4 time? Worst than that, to run 7/4, 7/4, then 8/4 and a chorus in 4/4 with seven measures instead of eight is insane and shows no adherence to traditional music theory or structure. It's a good thing that the record buying public didn't live by simple structure alone or they wouldn't have bought so many millions of copies.

Most people simply liked Beatles tunes and ninety nine percent of them will never know the real genius of their works; how they could ride the edge of the envelope and make it work each time with no formal training in their background. Most fans never knew that Lennon nor McCartney could read nor write music. They just knew what would work and experimented with key signatures and time signatures to produce masterpieces that few people in history could match.

The only other song that I can think of that used a 7/4 time signature was "Money" by Pink Floyd. It is so unique that it is still used in commercials around the world. Undoubtedly, that famous "Money' riff and the cash register sound effects made a huge impact, but the

7/4 time locks a missing beat feel in your head. It is reinforced when the guitar break changes to 4/4 then back to 7/4 again.

A music theorist would have a blast dissecting this song; a normal listener just knows that there is something intriguing about it but probably assumes that the magic is in the sound, not realizing the allure of the time signature.

"All You Need is Love" and "Money" are both loaded up with clever sound effects or unique interlacing of witty music pieces so how would one know if that is what made them both huge, timeless hits or if it was that missing note in the time signature. I would have loved to see them recorded clean to see if the time signature could have carried the songs without special effects.

To Each His Own

My sainted mother always said that the curse of the Irish is that the families fight too much. She thought that Irish families should stick together like Jewish families do.

I was able to see, early on, that there are unique characteristics to different ethnic groups.

Irish in the northeast are predominantly Democrats. Even though most are conservative as they age, they vote Democrat.

Irish families may be very loving but rarely show it through touching or hugging and rarely say I love you. Social occasions are normally based more on drink than food and the Irish would be the worst cooks in the world if not for the English.

Irish workers prefer public service or jobs with long term potential. Education was not considered the only way to progress in life.

Jews normally seek higher education. Jewish families drive education ideals into their children. Jewish families also foster an environment in which children can pursue their dreams, even if not overly pragmatic. This trait has helped to produce so many great comedians, musician, performers, writers, physicians, and academians. The tendency for Jews to assist family members to succeed has helped Jews to become the most successful ethnic group in America as well as most other Western countries. From Russia to Iran, economies would suffer greatly without Jews.

After the Inquisition, Spain, with all the riches of the New World, was unable to sustain success. Jews manage well.

Management is a strong Jewish trait. Although there are relatively few Jewish professional athletes, the sports managers, owners, agents, and attorneys are predominantly Jewish.

Jews are leaders in liberalism and socialist causes. Aside from the Kennedys, the leading liberals in the US are overwhelmingly Jewish. From Levin to Feinstein to Schumer to Boxer to Waxman, Liberal government leadership is disproportionately Jewish. In the Senate, ten out of thirteen Jewish senators are Democrats or Socialist. In the House twenty eight out of twenty nine are Democrats.

American Blacks are virtually exclusively Democrats. Blacks have a natural distrust of government. They are extremely loyal to Black causes whether they would normally believe in them or not. Most Blacks still back O.J. and Marion Berry regardless of evidence. Most Blacks will vote as Liberals but are Conservative in their private beliefs.

Black women are possibly the single strongest unit in America. They are the most resilient and resourceful survivors and are able to raise families through the most trying circumstances.

First generation Southeast Asians are some of the hardest working, and thrifty people in America today. Most will work ungodly hours to save enough money under a mattress to start a business, almost any business. Low interest rates are inherently important in purchases and taxes are something to be avoided at every opportunity.

Creature comforts are unimportant, except to many of the second generation who seem to have no trouble spending their parent's money as they assimilate into American society.

Although these are characterizations which are normally avoided in public conversation, people within these ethnic groups know these ethnic traits are fairly accurate. It makes ethnic groups unique and interesting. It also provides a tendency for groups to seek company in others of similar interests. Acknowledging these similarities is not bigotry, simply an understanding of distinctiveness.

Jack Gorman

To Outsource or
Not to Outsource

J ust a note about outsourcing. One area of outsourcing in concern is in the technical help received when someone needs assistance with a new computer or other high tech item.

When one calls the tech help number for assistance it may be answered at an office in India. These people chose to learn English as a second language AND learned enough about the product to offer the assistance required to satisfy the customer. This is also accomplished at a wage below American standard.

The alternative is to look inward for this skill. The American citizen who would generally expect such a wage would normally be found in the American inner city. The problem, as I perceive it however, is that many today do not find it socially acceptable to speak proper English and are far from being skilled enough to handle a customer's technical problems.

Imagine spending a thousand dollars or more on a new computer system, needing assistance with a problem which has frustrated you for hours, and then getting someone on the help line who is clueless. Would you consider it fair to receive inadequate help because the job was not outsourced? Or, would you be willing to pay additional money for tech help to speak with an American who was properly trained and enthusiastic to assist you.

Perhaps an option could be offered to call a more expensive DOMESTIC help line and the consumer could make the decision as to which line to call. Wouldn't you love to see the results!

Total Quality

A great concept! I had bought in lock, stock and barrel after a short study of it. It seemed like it was the savior of Japan and led them to dominate the world in the production of quality products.

The general concept is to under-promise and over-deliver; to turn out the highest quality product possible and to continuously strive to improve that product.

I had heard a story about 'total quality' as practiced by the Japanese who embraced it as a culture.

The story, factual or not, went like this. An American company was producing a high end product and needed to contract a particular electronic component to a Japanese company. The instructions were, that because it was to be used in the signature product line, the 10,000 components needed to be 97% error free. On the delivery date, two boxes arrived; one box with 10,000 components and another with 300 additional components. According to the story there was a note attached that said, "We hope that we satisfied the terms of the contract. In one box you will find 10,000 units, 100% error free. In the other you will find 300 additional units with errors. We're not sure why you wanted errors."

The story always gets the attention of people considering 'total quality' in their workplace. It infers that in a 'total quality' environment you would always strive for error free production. American companies who are not 'total quality' proponents have the bar set too low. Maybe this is why buyers prefer Lexus over American luxury cars. They never seem to break.

'Total Quality' seems like a no brainer. Cater to the customer – and everyone's a customer. There's internal customers, who could be your own employees, maybe your suppliers, etc. There's external customers, who would be the traditional customers; the people who buy your product.

It appears that, in Japan, this has developed and worked well for half a century. The one problematic component in the American system is the American customer. In the American culture, good service is sometimes considered a sign of weakness. Let a customer know that he is always right and he'll kick your butt. He'll want more and more till you finally reduce the quality of your product. A housewife will buy a product and abuse it because she knows that a 'total quality' organization will always take it back. It's our culture.

Municipal or union workers will not necessarily provide great service because they desire to provide a quality environment. Try to get a quality experience at a DMV office. Guaranteed job security is indirectly proportionate to good service.

I still like the concept of 'total quality'; it just doesn't seem to work well with real people.

True Campaign Reform

As an ordinary man my idea of presidential campaign reform seems very simple – stop the campaigning! Why are these people on the campaign trail anyway? The campaign trail, besides being obsolete, offers nothing more than an opportunity to lie to the voters; if not a direct lie, then an omission of the truth, or a twisting of words to deceive the public.

I recommend that, with virtually 100% of the voting public having access to TV, computers, radio, or newspapers, the candidates address their points directly to the voters.

Live, on TV, radio, and bit streamed they can present their platform individually, then debate, and then repeat the process on a weekly basis starting sixty days prior to November.

A cable station and over the air station can be made available every four years strictly for this purpose to eliminate network partisanship. I would also hope that people who did not view the presentations would refrain from voting.

Campaign advertising should be eliminated so the voters will have equal exposure to each candidate.

One major advantage is that all lies, deceptions, and false promises not caught during the debate can be identified, investigated and addressed the following week directly to the voters.

The list of benefits is huge:

1. It will reduce the partisan influence of the news media.
2. No more ACORN.
3. No unanswered accusations.

4. Third parties can be represented.
5. Campaigners can continue working their jobs till the election.
6. Reduce the ridiculous two years of campaigning as is done now.
7. All points and promises can be contested and defended the following week.
8. Campaigning costs can be handled by the two bucks deducted from our tax returns.
9. Campaign contributions become obsolete.
10. The American public sees who is running and hears their pitch directly.
11. Foreign money influence is reduced.
12. Lobbyists are reduced.

The current process of TV ads spouting lies or filling football stadiums with cheering crowds of people who are either pundits or unemployed people who would be better off procuring a job where they could spend their time earning a decent living to support themselves and their families rather than following a candidate around like a rock star groupie, does nothing to select the best candidate for the job.

Why should presidential campaigning continue to be done as a circus act in the 21st Century?

Tell me where I'm wrong or how this could be implemented.

Two Party System

Our Founding Fathers somehow knew that a Party System would cause problems in the future. It's amazing how they predicted the future so accurately in so many ways. Washington's Farewell Address warned about the dangers of a two party system. I believe that one of his concerns was the opening of the door for foreign interests to influence our government through the parties.

It has progressed so far today that there is no backing up. The parties have taken complete control of our government and allow for no other input at all. No one from outside the two parties can ever contribute to the good of the nation. What a waste of talent! One must follow the accepted doctrine of one party or the other and if not, can never be recognized.

The result is zealots for leaders. Zealots back zealots and fund zealots while normal people simply go to work day to day and raise their families. This is probably not what our Founding Fathers proposed.

This system forces people onto one team or the other. Not necessarily fostering the good of the nation, but protecting the party line.

There are basic differences among people's beliefs; such as whether one's allegiance should be to America or the world for example. These are inherent differences in core conviction and should not be classified into one of the two parties. Because each nuance has had to be placed in one party or the other there is no longer an ala carte option for the citizens. One must select from one menu or the other completely and exclusively.

The two party system has evolved to the point where voters must vote a party line over an American line, forcing the needs of the party above the needs of the country.

Candidates who follow the party line have the only chance of success because most campaign funding is provided by the DNC and RNC. Alienation from these funding sources eliminates any chance of success.

Instead of growing out of this paradigm during the past two hundred years it has become so firmly entrenched that it may become the mainstay till the end of U.S. history.

We Close at Nine

"**O**ur registers will be closing in ten minutes. Please bring your purchases to the checkout". Great words which are greatly appreciated by employees who have put in a full day's work and are anxious to get home to their families.

Now, let's return to the rest of the world. The waitress and bus boy who watch the customer run inside the restaurant door at 8:59 are contemplating spitting in the food of these thoughtless, inconsiderate, customers. Yes, technically, the restaurant is still open but it is open for thoughtful, considerate customers to finish their meals. The 8:59'er is also the one who spends the most time perusing the menu, expects perfect service and will nurse a cup of coffee forever. In the kitchen, the cooks are on hold for cleanup because the inconsiderate maggots at the table don't care about anyone but themselves. The ovens stay on, the fryers can't be cleaned and the dishwasher can't be run. The cook, the cleanup crew, the waitress, the bus boy, and the manager sacrifice time with their families so that some thoughtless clowns can run a $30.00 tab and leave a $5.00 tip.

If you are the 8:59'er, please take this personally. It's about you, and you are that thoughtless, inconsiderate bastard who doesn't even realize how many times you have dined on other people's spit; and you deserve it. If you have been doing it out of ignorance – change!

When you show up at 8:59 to the car dealership, understand that those people have been there for over twelve hours and will hit hour thirteen and fourteen as you cutely scan the color charts and decide on all your options. The salesman may appear enthusiastic but that's his job. He's simply being polite to someone who didn't take the time to plan a proper schedule; to someone who elected to go to dinner first so that the salesman will miss his dinner. As you enjoy the excitement of the negotiations a cleanup crew is waiting out back to clean up your shiny new car, the finance manager is waiting so he can enjoy the pleasure of your company, the sales manager is waiting, and the janitors are on hold so as not to interrupt you, the customer. Because they are treating you like royalty, believe me, it's only because it's their job. During normal store hours they are very glad to see you and they actually have job satisfaction by watching you enjoy your new purchase. After hours, you are an inconsiderate bother. A professional business has posted hours which should be respected. When you don't respect them, you are not respected. You are a thoughtless lout.

In the car business this is sometimes the case with customers who believe that they will get the best bargain if they can pressure the sales staff after hours. Most of the time it is simply selfish personalities.

My respect goes to the store that announces that the cashiers will close in ten minutes.

What Happened to Military Credit?

O ne thing that was always a sure bet was the credit rating of a GI. Even with fixed incomes, and not much of it, GIs could make purchases based on their excellent credit and the knowledge that a creditor could always collect from a GI because mismanagement of personal affairs was not tolerated in the military.

One personal encounter occurred a number of years ago while I was active duty. One of my subordinates had a creditor contact our squadron commander regarding a debt owed by his wife. She had been scammed into a photo developing scheme to have 400 pictures a month developed under a lifetime contract. As she realized that she wouldn't need 400 pictures per month any longer she attempted to get out of the contract. To pressure her into paying, the company contacted her husband's commander.

I was instructed to present my troop with a non-judicial punishment form for failing to properly manage his family. That's how serious the military was about the public reputation of military members.

As a side note, I refused to administer the Article 15 because I perceived the problem to be between his wife and a crooked photo company. This didn't play all too well with my career, as the XO was not desiring to look bad in front of the commander and questioned my ability to be a 'team player'.

Although this was an extreme case, it is just an example of how seriously the military considered the management of personal affairs.

Fast forward to today. A large percentage of younger troops couldn't buy a cup of coffee at McDonalds with a two dollar down payment. Their credit is so torn up that they will probably never own a home of their own. The interest rate for a car, at their own credit union, may be over 15%. The troops are making much more money than ever before and are not paying their bills. Their commanders aren't paying their own bills either in many cases.

The only sure bet for great credit is with the older GIs who are still members of the old school.

For the younger troops, the only place that they can go for a loan, a good number of times, is their own military credit union who will take the money automatically from their paycheck.

What happened? Maybe the following story can explain part of it. I was speaking with a Navy Chief about a situation he had experienced a short while ago. While on sea trials, they ran an exercise simulating an attack and he directed a young sailor below deck to help out in the engine room. Instead of reporting as ordered, the sailor pulled a 'stress card' from his pocket and requested time in his bunk to rest. The real stress in that situation was the frustration of the Chief of not being able to throw the sailor overboard.

Who's to say whether the old military methods were better than the new military methods? The military personnel do seem to have their credit worsened today. Maybe there will be a happy medium.

What if Hendrix Played Guitar Hero

G uitar hero is a video game where kids get a chance to play a make believe guitar, to make believe that they are part of a band. The Guitar Hero guitar has no strings, just colored buttons which you are to press in time with colored lights which flash on the TV screen in coordination with music played in the program. There is no music knowledge required and no new music written by the player. You simply hit a button when the program tells you to, to make believe that you are a musician. The game appears to be a lot of fun because many kids are addicted to it.

Thank God that Hendrix was never introduced to Guitar Hero. If he had chosen that, there would have been no Hendrix. He would never have written any of his rock classics, never performed in concert, and the rock world would have been worse off for it. He would have sat in his bedroom pressing buttons to someone else's music. Nothing is created nor recorded. No music knowledge is required and music is finished any further progression.

Video games are so entertaining that millions of kids are absolutely addicted to them. These kids are sitting by their selves, reacting to a game which was written by someone that they have never met and will never know. The player will create nothing for anyone else to ever see or hear. When the game is over, all the brain bytes of the player are lost. No record, and no improvement for the world exists.

Prior to video games, many kids occupied themselves by learning to play instruments, learning to paint, or maybe to sculpt.

Luckily, Michelangelo had no video games so he was forced to occupy his time with art which enriched the world. His paintings and sculptures endure.

A result of the video game revolution is that today there are virtually no classical instrument players. It is much more fun to fight dragons on a TV screen than to study the bassoon or French horn. The next generation may never see a symphony orchestra performed by live musicians on real instruments. There won't be enough musicians or conductors to perform.

There may never be another Jimmy Page or Brian May or B.B. King because few kids are taking the time and discipline to learn to play the guitar because there is instant gratification from Guitar Hero without even having to learn how to tune a guitar.

The classics will truly be the classics because no more will be created. Kids will simply make believe that they are playing along with the music that was already created by people who, thank God, had no video games in their formulative years.

What is Owed to Deliberate Non-performers?

S ome groups today have decided to revel in their ignorance and have established an elevated status by feigning a rebellion to intelligent English usage when, in fact, most have never acquired an acceptable ability to communicate in the language. Their intention is to diminish the fact that they were not willing to work hard enough to obtain a working knowledge of our language when offered the opportunity, free of charge, in public school.

Their insinuation is that they possess the ability to communicate in English, however, they choose to sound ignorant to reflect a unique identity.

The fact that this unique identity alienates most potential employers only compounds the self imposed discrimination problem which leads so many of the followers of this cult to remain in a poverty environment and eventually demand compensation from those who have prospered through hard work, and compliance to the rules of success.

To people who communicate in standard English, the intentional 'dumbing down' of the language sounds ignorant, and often even threatening, as the icons of the dialect are often self described gangsters who profit, and prophet, through the implication of violence and anarchy.

The question is, what is owed to these people as they fail to thrive in this society? As they age and become a burden on taxpayers who have worked to succeed while the 'cultists' have played their roles as gangsters, and then victims; as they impregnate and then abandon, what do the hard working citizens owe these people? What does the ant owe the grasshopper?

This type of question seems to be the dividing point of Liberals and Conservatives. Setting aside the exceptions, where there are truly victims due to no fault of their own, is there valid debate as to the existence of those who purposely choose to bypass the opportunities of becoming productive members of society in lieu of their perceived path to glory as a gangster?

Are all gangsters simply victims of an unfair society whose purpose is to intentionally shackle the unfortunates? If so, then just compensation may indeed be reparations from the public treasury.

On the other hand, if this lifestyle is intentionally selected by a conscious decision to disregard the consequences for the immediate gratification of a 'gangster life', then the cost should be borne solely by the decision maker.

If these are the platforms of Liberals vs. Conservatives then choose a side. If your choice can be defended then there is a distinct and definite division which can never be breached.

What Makes Music?

Two verses, a chorus then repeat. That's the formula for a successful pop song. It's been that way for over half a century. It's what the listener expects. The drummer does a change-up and vocal harmonies strengthen the chorus because, more often than not, the chorus sells the song.

There are certain patterns that are common in most successful songs. One standard is the I-IV-I-V-IV-I which is used so often in the blues. This means that the chord progression, in say the key of A, would be: A D A E D A. This one, or slight variations of it, was used in many rock and roll songs for years. Probably 30% of your favorite songs follow this progression. It works for ballads or rockers and lets a kid write a hit song with only three chords in his repertoire.

To sexy up a ballad there are some great progressions that are so simple but so distinct that writers like Buddy Holly and Burton Cummings have made a living from them. You can hear these in ballads like 'Laughing' from the Guess Who, where the 5th of the I chord is augmented and augmented and augmented before going to the IV which is then minored. It's a beautiful run which you can hear in a ton of great ballads.

Another great one in this vein is the diminishing of the bass note of the I chord till it leads to the II chord minored. Or, augmenting the 5th note of the base chord to lead you to the II chord minored. These progressions are magic and just playing with them will bring 100 classics to mind.

256 | JACK GORMAN

A real beauty is the walk down bass progression in songs like 'A Whiter Shade of Pale'. It lets a root of three basic chords produce a monster hit.

From the middle of the 50's, on, all budding piano players and guitarists learned one extra chord so they could play the C-Am-F-G progression like they heard in 'Heart and Soul' and then in so many ballads. Learning that Am turned scrub musicians into accomplished musicians who could play most of the Dion and Ritchie Valens hits.

To really throw lust into a song the next step was to work with the maj7. This had been used to add a certain feel to songs like 'The Girl from Ipanema', but by augmenting that 7th it gave an ending chord to any ballad, that made girls cry. Used on the base chords during a song it gives that lustful sound as is heard in 'The Sun Ain't Gonna Shine Anymore' or 'Best of My Love'. It gives almost a minor feel to a song written in a major mode.

Minor variations like these have added the color to music which has made music such a major part of most people's lives. The clever manipulation of twelve notes has added more pleasure to the world than almost anything else but . . .

When God Designed Music

The day God designed music was a glorious day. As He pondered it's correlation to man and made His final plans, He really out did Himself. Although the design would give Him millions of years of enjoyment just watching the random development complement His programmed music; it also turned out to be one of His greatest gifts to mankind.

He was initially toying with the idea of just enjoying song birds, whale songs, and the other beautiful sounds of nature. When He decided to incorporate mankind into the music equation it was a 'win win'.

To let man do a proper job of it He saw the need for an upgraded brain to handle the complex math required for rhythm and harmony. I believe that God had decided to put this math function in a separate processor so that it would not interfere with the normal math functions required for day to day demands of a brain.

If you think about it, the music portion of the brain could be an extreme drain on the processor. Basic rhythms alone could draw too much of the available brain power[5].

Think about the demands. To a basic rhythm add a tone and keep it mathematically on pitch. Add a second, third, and consecutive tones of varying pitch that can be repeated and varied to make an interesting and pleasing tune that can be remembered and duplicated at another time; and, by another person.

---

[5]   This is why a person can tap his foot to a song and still perform another function.

To this, add lyrics that are meaningful to the performer and listener and make them rhyme. Add instruments to accompany the voice, such as percussion which will hold a beat and allow for others with percussion instruments to join in using variations of the same math formula to allow interesting patterns which complement each other[6].

Other instruments can be added with which the brain can procure the pitch of the desired song and duplicate it and harmonize with it to make an even more pleasing product.

As you can see, the math processor for such a function must be enormous.

Fortunately, God foresaw the future and prepared well. He allowed for beautiful, complicated music with intricate harmonies and the incorporation of elaborate instruments, symphony orchestras, choirs, recording capabilities, and on, and on, and on. It is beyond me to guess what the future holds in store for music. How could an ancient Greek lute player imagine a Beethoven symphony? How could Mozart imagine a $200 Yamaha keyboard with all the sounds of a symphony orchestra? How could Lennon and McCartney with only a two track recorder imagine a 24 channel, digital portable studio sitting in the bedroom of a budding musician today?

The products that were turned out throughout history prove the capabilities of the human brain: the giant chorale pieces from Bach, done without a single tape recorder; Beethoven worked without even having the ability to hear.

As amazing as they were, it continues today as modern musicians, composers, and recording engineers handle huge pieces of music for movies, CD sales, and whatever else requires music for people's, (and God's) enjoyment.

All this is based on the simple math processor that God had the forethought to include in the human brain. Thanks!

This does beg another question. Does God really know all? Maybe he left some surprises for Himself to see what man would do with this music option. I hope He likes it. What's He think of rap?

---

[6]   Picture the great rhythms of Santana with congas, timbales, cabasas, etc. working with the drummer.

When It's Yeller Leave It Meller

When it's yeller leave it meller; when it's brown flush it down. This was part of my indoctrination, as a homeowner with a septic system, from my ninety year old neighbor in upstate New York. It was up in God's country where the long winters with months of frozen ground made access to your septic system almost impossible.

That was his way of imparting wisdom in life's fundamentals. Never having been challenged by septic systems myself, the impact was not realized till it was too late. My family had always flushed a toilet whenever it was used. This was not the way of the wise in that neck of the woods.

The first consequence of too much flushing was the need to pump out the septic tank. Unfortunately, the access cover was a foot under the frozen ground which required me to chisel a chip at a time, for hours, at ten below zero until the cover was completely clear for the pump truck. Pumping is preferably done in the summer time.

The motivation to chisel was the loss of all sewage usage which included not just toilets, but sinks, and washing machines also. In a house with kids, that is quite a burden and a burden which would have had to have been endured till spring when the ground thawed. To make matters worse, pumping out the tank was not a permanent fix.

When the ground did thaw, a whole new leech field was required meaning no back yard for the kids that year.

Funny how being a bit more conservative in septic system use can make such a huge difference.

Almost thirty years later I still remember the words of advice, "when it's yeller leave it meller; when it's brown flush it down.

The real lesson learned – make sure you buy a house with city sewage.

When the Music Clicks

There's a magic in making music that only a small percentage of the world has ever truly experienced. In the rock world it is when the band is in synch and the rest of the world disappears. There's an elevated plateau where the players become part of a team and share thoughts at a level where each knows the thoughts of the other and can feel where the music needs to go next. When it's clicking, the band all have the same roadmap in their heads as opposed to symphony orchestra players who have the roadmap in the sheet music in front of them.

When you listen to Clapton's 'Layla', you can feel the interaction of Duane Allman's slide guitar on the band. The band compliments his work and you can almost experience the rapport among the players. It's strong when it's needed and decrescendos as a single unit to make the song perfect. That's why the song has lasted all these years.

When you tour the famous studio 'B' in Nashville, the guide elaborates on this concept. When Elvis recorded there he utilized the magic. That magic was what made one room in one building produce over a thousand hits.

When Elvis reserved the room he did it at night. Even though the room was in high demand, and extremely expensive to use, he spent the hours setting the stage for the magic. He would order in food for everyone involved, set everyone at ease and would jam with the Jordanaires, impromptu, on the Steinway. All with no pressure. He spent three quarters of his recording time not recording. As he intimated with the musicians he established the rapport that was about to make perfection.

It's why his music clicked and why you can feel it in his recordings. Whether you're an Elvis fan or not, there's no denying the magic. Studio 'B' provided the atmosphere which allowed the magic to occur. It allowed musicians to click.

All this goes to show the importance of clicking. It provides a euphoria which others try to find in drugs. Many musicians also used drugs in an attempt to lengthen the period of magic which sometimes only lasts as long as the three minute song; while the harmonies are perfect, the drummer and bass are in perfect time and each player knows he's in the zone.

In the music world most people only get a chance to witness the results by listening to the recording. The lucky few are the musicians who provide the recordings which manifest the few short minutes of greatness that occur every once in a while when the players become one and the result is a product which is greater than the sum of its parts.

It seems that, today, there are fewer and fewer real musicians. In places like New York City where there are eight million potential musicians there are no garages to practice in. In rural areas, the selection of 'perfect matches' is limited by the limited number of potentially gifted musicians. Musicians tend to feed off each other to achieve greatness such as Lennon and McCartney and Simon and Garfunkel.

A great musician in a band can elevate the other players to their optimum but that optimum must be exceptional or the bar is set too low for greatness. Freddie Mercury may have been an exceptional writer and performer but teamed with Brian May, Roger Taylor and John Deacon, the synergy culminated in one of the greatest British bands in history.

Clapton spent a lifetime searching for like minded musicians to experience the magic. Because the magic was in such short supply he was forced to resort to chemical substitution in an attempt to duplicate the feeling.

I wonder if all this is the reason for the success of the video game 'Rock Band'. The game lets a kid become a playing member of a rock band as a singer, guitarist, or drummer. There's no need to learn to play a real instrument or read music. You simply play along with professional song tracks. The developers provided the challenge of hitting a particular note, or drum at a particular time so that the player feels that there is a challenge and a reward. The purpose is to provide the feeling of playing as a contributing member a real rock band.

It is an extremely popular game and maybe will entice kids to actually learn to play a real instrument to maybe become a real musician and expand beyond the make believe world of video games. Until a kid experiences his first euphoric experience as a real musician he will never truly know the magic.

Where Do We Stand in the World?

W here does the United States really stand in the world? It is very clear from the accounts of the news media that our standing is very low in the eyes of the world. We are led to believe that the world believes that they would be better off without the interference of the U.S. Having traveled the world a bit, as well as having a fair knowledge of world history, I tend to doubt the reports.

I do acknowledge that idealists around the world occasionally protest U.S. positions and actions however; most realists in the free world hold a different opinion, even if it is rarely manifested.

The benefits that we provide the world are enormous. Take, for example, the fact that Ireland maintains virtually no standing army. Offering no possible resistance to British occupation of all of Ireland, U.S. opinion, alone, provides the security which has allowed Irish peace and prosperity in the Free State since the 1920's.

Africa's population loss from AIDS and malaria has been greatly reduced due to U.S. aid. U.S. education and training opportunities have also provided many third world nations with avenues to prosperity.

Millions of Muslims throughout the ex-Soviet Union world now practice their faith without government oppression only because of U.S. actions.

A North Korean threat to South Korea is held at bay mainly because of us, and the growth of human rights and prosperity in China would not exist without the existence of the U.S.

Our assistance in the rebuilding of our former enemies, Japan and Germany, has allowed both to assume peaceful power positions in the economic world.

If France were to be threatened by Russia, who would be expected to step up to the plate, even though they show no respect for us?

People prospering in peace in Poland, the Czech and Slovak republics, Lithuania, Estonia, the former East Germany, Ukraine, and the 'stan countries should remember their position compared to their parents' and say a prayer for the continued power of the U.S. Why wasn't Georgia crushed by Russia? Were Switzerland and Belgium a deterrent to Putin?

The desire of left wing Americans to succumb to world pressures to disarm, to de-nuke, and to emulate the Europeans would not just reduce our own security but would threaten the security and prosperity of much of the world who are threatened by those who do not play well with others.

If we reduced our military size and strength to that proportion that exists in Switzerland how long would the free nations of the world exist? What would the future hold for Israel? Why don't U.S. Jews understand this before they vote so idealistically?

How long could we exist as a free nation if our security was directly dependent upon the forces of the U.N.?

I believe that the rest of the world should do a periodic check up and give thanks for the freedoms they possess due to the strength of the U.S.

Who Controls the Election?

Just to belabor my paranoia, as an ordinary man, I get curious sometimes about what lies beneath the surface of this election. I had been thinking that the powers behind the left control the election results by damaging our economy then providing 'change' as our salvation. I was thinking how *lucky* it was for them that the housing market crashed bringing down Wall Street and crushing the 'common people' just prior to the election.

I normally would look to George Soros to be behind such a feat, in that he is an anti-Republican zealot, AND, he had done it to England in the past.

Looking into Soros' associates, one noteworthy one is Herb Sandler who was instrumental in the bundling of bad real estate mortgages and then reselling them to screw the market for a huge personal profit. *FYI, this is the one that Saturday Night Live was not allowed to spoof.* Maybe it wasn't luck at all.

One of their connections is through 'America Votes' (if you have any suspicion at all that this may be true, look up americavotes.org).

As our attention is on the election as it appears on the surface, the loss of all three branches of our government holds more consequence than anyone but the Soros crowd knows.

I doubt that Obama nor his grass roots followers have put the pieces of the puzzle together. I don't think that their desires and the Soros intentions are the same.

Soros is pushing 80 years old and his goals of subordinating the US to the world are either accomplished soon or he won't experience the result.

As Republicans concentrate on problems like ACORN, which I believe is simply an organization breaking the rules for racial purposes, I think that the true danger to our sovereignty is being missed.

Do some quick reading on what Soros did to England causing 'black Wednesday' in '92 then re-read this piece.

As the market was crumbling why did it crash a month before the election? Why was 'change' established as a slogan a year before the election? Could a rational thinker think that this wasn't planned?

Who Do You Work For?

A subject that is hot on the minds of Americans today is Unions. The battles from days of old, between union workers and management still loom over Detroit and many other manufacturing cities. They may be the cause for the threat to our automobile empire.

The people are asking why the Japanese companies in America are faring so well while the Domestics are dying? The answer may come down to how a worker responds to a direct question: who do you work for?

For Japanese companies in the US such as Honda or Canon the answer to the question is surely – Honda, or Canon. Asking a Ford worker may elicit a different answer such as the U.A.W.

When you work for a company there may be a question of 'product pride' when you believe that the nameplate represents you, and is a symbol of your good work.

It may also be part of the reason why so few workers call in sick with foreign nameplates. The purpose of a union has evolved to the point that some believe that their job security is guaranteed; similar to tenure in the education world. That feeling of assuredness enhances the allegiance to the union which will fight your battle with the company whether you are right of wrong.

A result is that many union companies are forced to over-man to cover Mondays and Fridays when workers are more likely to call in sick. This all goes into the overall cost of production.

Another result is that many buyers seem to prefer to purchase 'non-union' products because they believe that the quality is better.

Unions have come a long way from their original purpose.

I asked an old timer, yesterday, who he had worked for. His answer was Bethlehem Steel. Good answer! I believe that America has always made the finest steel in the world. Try to wear out a Leatherman.

He truly, and righteously, believed that he always produced the highest quality steel possible. That's possibly what is missing in the American auto industry.

Who Should Be Able to Send American Soldiers to War?

T he commander in chief is the president of the United States but congress declares war.

Question – As commander in chief should the president be required to have a vested stake in the decision to forfeit American lives? Should the President have at least had active duty experience to have empathy for the troops?

The Constitution requires civilian control over the military, but where is the true understanding of the grave consequences of a bad decision? Without ever having been there how can someone in the White House be qualified to make such a decision?

How about congress in the decision to declare war? Should only members who are veterans vote on such decisions or should these voters be required to have their own kids or grand kids on active duty for the duration of the war. The perception has normally been that these decisions are made by grey haired old men who probably have money invested in corporations which will profit from war. American decision makers, hopefully, would never profit financially from any such decision. Repercussions should be more than severe.

My opinion is that 'war' should never have to be declared. [7] The verbal contest of 'conflict' versus 'war' has always been a sore point

---

[7] The Viet Nam 'Conflict' with the loss of over fifty thousand American lives has inflicted so much unnecessary grief on so many Americans because of semantics (my apologies to any readers under 40 who probably wouldn't remember this).

with me. If American interests are so threatened that it would require a military response, then the response should be quick and devastating. Troop deployment beyond 'special forces' should mean that America's survivability is at stake and that there are no more bombers available. This, to me, is the distinction between conflict and war. One or two successful conflicts could eliminate the potential of any future war. Childhood experience has shown most people that assholes rarely picked on the toughest kid in the class. America is the toughest kid in the class. We just have decided to hide that fact. Even the loss of thousands of American lives has not enticed us to acknowledge our true position.

I believe that the unbelievable amount of American blood that has been sacrificed from the Revolutionary War till now has justified this decision.

So, who should be able to send American soldiers to war? To conflict – the President as per Article 2, Section 2 of the Constitution, with the Senate and House Armed Services Committees (my recommendation). Note! The selection of Armed Services Committee members should almost require a prerequisite of military experience or family commitment (my recommendation). One must have a 'dog in the fight'!

To war – Congress, as per Article 1, Section 8 of the Constitution. This is a huge decision and deserves the thorough application of experience, debate, and review of 535 members. The Founding Fathers meant to make it difficult!

Whoever Gets to Grandma First

There's been a funny societal metamorphosis in the past twenty years. In the retail world of big ticket items, namely cars, the rule used to be: whoever gets to Grandma first gets the car.

What this means is: for a young buyer with no credit, or bad credit, a cosigner is required. Because the nut doesn't fall far from the tree today, Mom often had bad credit also.

In the past there was Grandma. Grandma came from a time when your credit rating was your reputation. Good credit told the world of your status. It was equal to your 'word', your 'bond'. Grandma paid cash when possible and borrowed only what was necessary. Loans were paid on time, every time. The result was perfect credit scores for Grandma.

This did not always pass to the next generation, and definitely not to today's generation. For whatever reason, neither generation learned anything from Grandma. The call for material goods generally overrides good sense today.

When a young woman wanted to buy a car it was normally a vehicle far beyond their budget, with zero down payment, and no bank in the world would lend under such conditions. Mom was normally willing to cosign but often had credit that was worse than the daughter's.

The answer was Grandma. The trick was to get to Grandma first. Whoever got to Grandma first got the car. Whoever got there second got nothing because whoever had gotten there first rarely paid their car payment on time and ended up killing Grandma's credit.

This concept of getting Grandma to cosign does not work today because today's Grandma is often yesterday's Mom who had no credit ethics, most of the good Grandmas have been used up *and*, the banks have wised up to the routine.

Why would any salesman send a young buyer after Grandma when he knew the inevitable outcome? Because the experienced salesman knew that that young buyer was going to get a car that day, whether it was from him or from another dealer.

Where have the real grandmas gone?

Why the Need for Strong Leadership

Watching the battles of our next potential leaders I an amazed at the charisma of the candidates and the political success of the charm factor. The concern that I have is the ability of these darlings of diplomacy when they are confronting real men.

At Yalta, a sickly FDR and an aging Churchill, bent on diplomacy, confronted Joseph Stalin and got their asses kicked. Stalin was from the streets of Georgia and had fought his way to the top through cunning, intimidation, and the killing of opposition.

His overpowering of FDR and Churchill fostered a 'cold war' which lasted for half a century and permitted countless deaths throughout the Soviet Union and Europe.

Neville Chamberlain met his match while dealing with Hitler. Counting on diplomacy and good faith, Hitler interpreted Chamberlain as a weakling leader of shopkeepers. The result of this mismatch was catastrophic.

So many foreign leaders had not progressed to the top through wealth, privilege, or charm. Unlike the beauty contest that is becoming the road to American political success. The Bin Ladens, the Castros, and the Mugabes of the world never even lose sleep over the deaths of thousands who stood in their way.

Picturing Yeltsin standing down a revolution in front of the Kremlin by daring a soldier to put a bullet through him shows what kind of guts many of these leaders have.

Khrushchev badgered Kennedy into believing that Russia would launch ICBMs on us even though they probably didn't have a workable delivery system. Banging his shoe on the desk at the UN like a madman gained a lot of headway in a room full of educated gentlemen who were intimidated by this show.

I wonder how US leadership would stand up against these types of personalities. Even piss ant leaders today will threaten to bury countries such as Israel which could have major repercussions on us.

Could the leader of an American 'beauty contest' election fend well for us against such adversaries? Could you picture him, or her, staring down a tank to protect the Whitehouse as Yeltsen did for the Kremlin?

To compete successfully for the US Executive position, one must promise more free stuff than his competitors and must also promise to ensure the rights of America's enemies. If you don't believe this, just review the candidate's platforms. Remember, if an American city is in dire jeopardy and the perpetrator is in custody; the rights of the terrorist are equal to the lives of a million American citizens.

The most 'civil' leader is in greatest demand in the US. Britain has led the way with this and we're working hard to catch up. Hey, didn't they used to be called Great Britain?

My Thoughts on Why We're So Fat

Two items that I blame for much of the obesity today are artificial sweeteners and carbonation. Unfortunately, they combine in diet soda. Have you ever seen a fat person without a diet coke?

I believe that artificial sweeteners trick the body into believing that sugar has been consumed and the pancreas reacts to control it. Without the sugar to act upon, the insulin is in excess which may be as harmful as being too low.

Carbonation gives a bloated feeling which makes the stomach muscles relax to reduce the discomfort. The worst thing to do is to relax stomach muscles which become more and more critical to tight abs, especially as one gets older. The gas in the stomach also leaves an empty feeling when it leaves, making you feel prematurely hungry.

Diet carbonated drinks are so prevalent today because people believe that they are helping them to lose weight. The flavors are so addictive that most people lose their taste for non-diet drinks. The future will show that these drinks are the cause of many additional problems.

I do wish that I was a renowned scientist so that I could publish my theories and clean up on a lucrative research grant. The diet drink people might offer me even more money to withhold my discoveries.

World Without Gas Engines

What would the world be like without internal combustion engines? Almost everything about our daily lives is a result of our current transportation modes which allow homes to be located far from work, goods to be produced thousands of miles from consumers, and absolute mobility for everyone. Our transportation system is based on internal combustion engines.

Acceptance of this type of transport established the need for the present day road systems which cater to individual vehicular use. Most of the goods transported throughout the country are carried by individual trucks which are sharing the roads with individually owned cars, motorcycles, SUVs, and trucks.

This is all possible because some brilliant engineers had developed gas engines prior to 1900. The concept was as old as the thirteenth century but it was not in production until the late nineteenth century.

Once the engine worked, it became the accepted standard and nothing else received any significant attention. The engine has continuously been improved and in the last couple of decades the Japanese have tweaked it till it may very well be as efficient as it will ever be. Even at its optimum, it is still not adequate to keep us off imported oil.

This one invention has set the standard for almost everything we do in life today. Most of us ride one person to a car and spend massive amounts of our income on vehicle ownership, insurance, and fuel. Many of us spend hours per day commuting to and from work and this is also related to affordable individual ownership of vehicles, made possible by the internal combustion engine.

What if there was no internal combustion engine? What if it never became the standard? What if no one put the pieces together? What if oil was not so readily available that everyone could afford to own cars?

Some of the larger cities come close to this scenario. Subways, trolleys, monorails, and even watercraft substitute for automobiles.

Without individual ownership of millions and millions of cars there would be no need for such an elaborate system of highways, streets, tunnels, and bridges. People would probably work and shop much closer to home. Electric, steam, or nuclear may be powering large, public transportation which would have become much more efficient, user friendly and maybe even run on time.

Barge travel was once very popular in the US and Britain using canal systems which allowed huge amounts of cargo to be moved by mules and horses. The canals are still in use in England by vacationers and the Intercoastal Waterway has been in use on the US east coast since colonial times.

Without the internal combustion engine our whole way of life would be different.

Steam engines which are more adapted for large transport such as locomotives may also have been perfected and in common use if not for competition from gas powered engines.

Electric bikes and Segway types of transport would undoubtedly be in popular use. Whatever cars and trucks that did exist would be electric or hydrogen and all of the research that had been spent on gas engines would have been invested in perfecting these. Even if never achieving the efficiency of gasoline powered internal combustion engines, they would at least be at optimum efficiency by now without the competition for the research dollars which have traditionally been spent on the gas engine.

Funny enough, we might even have space travel because rocket propulsion is not based on reciprocating engines. Neither are jets.

Given the time, I could probably write a book on the prospects of no gasoline engines.

As long as gas engines are available and affordable, there will be little viable competition.

Would You Give Up Your Rights?

One thing that my mother preached to me was to never give up any rights. Being a lifelong Democrat, she had some mixed messages. One right that she felt strong about was the right to bear arms. Although she would never desire to own a gun, it was a right, and once gone, would never be granted again.

With that entrenched in my soul since childhood, I did come upon a perplexing situation. While parked outside an elementary school in Newport News, Virginia, I was astonished with the brazen crime not twenty five yards from the fence surrounding the school.

In the housing projects courtyard, in broad daylight, there were drug transactions taking place. The criminal element was fearless.

Knowing many of the police in town I have had the opportunity to discuss this a number of times. It is understood that that area is virtually an 'untouchable' zone. Drugs, weapons, and prostitution are not uncommon. The girls in section 8 housing have live-in boyfriends but a blind eye is turned. There is a balance there that the police are not anxious to upset.

Even though it is directly across from a school, there is little that can be done.

It seems, to an ordinary man, that there should be plenty that can be done. Video cameras during the day and a curfew at night could provide safety to the law abiding residents but both may be violating one's rights.

Declaring a 'no gun' zone and maybe implementing a no loitering, vagrancy, or soliciting policy, except for legal residents, may also provide a better living environment for the kids who should have a right to safely play in the area. Again, as in so many low income – high crime communities around the country, this is not done.

This begs the question: what rights would you be willing to forego for the well being of the community? Would you agree to an after-dark curfew? Would you agree to be searched for weapons and drugs? Would you agree to an ID card?

How about if these restrictions were for a finite period of time and were enforced by the police to eliminate the dangerous vagrants?

In many affluent communities these rights are already compromised for the good of the community and the protection of the inhabitants. Many communities are gated and restrict noise, décor, solicitation, etc.

Is it anymore of a freedoms violation in the projects than in an upscale development? Why does it seem that it is less tolerated in the projects although it would provide more than a nicer standard of living; it could save lives?

Yoko Ono

J ust another opinion, but I think that the darkest day in the history of Rock and Roll was the day that John Lennon met Yoko Ono. From everything I have read she sucked the life out of him for the sole purpose of controlling him and attempting to become part of something greater than she could ever have been on her own.

The accounts of the friction that she caused among the Beatles were pretty consistent from most of the people who had witnessed it. Her control over John by aggravating his addictions is legendary.

As she inserted herself into his music, her banshee-like screeching must have turned Paul's stomach as he saw the Beatles disintegrating. She must have known that even John Lennon couldn't make a no talent hag into a star.

Interviews that I have heard on BBC with those involved with the White Album revealed a distain for Yoko. Most noteworthy was during a recording session where she desired to screech on the recording and questioned the engineer's ability to properly record it.

What a terrible loss for Rock and Roll, the day she entered onto the scene.

Additional Rants Brought on by My Personal Distaste for a Biased and Reckless Media.

60 Minutes Does it Again 9/08

Sunday night's 60 Minutes did it again. First hand reporting on how the US Air Force is targeting innocent civilians in Afghanistan. They reported in depth about 2000 lb bombs being authorized to be dropped on a house containing nine family members. Although men were spotted entering the house with weapons there were no traces of them by the time the military examined the remains.

Downplayed was the fact that the residents were aware of the house being used by Taliban killers to attack American forces.

Because the Taliban was unsuccessful in their attempt to kill our soldiers, the defensive retaliation was considered excessive.

60 Minutes even managed to interview the surviving child who now hates Americans. How much could he and his family have loved Americans while the Taliban was operating from their home. The love was not enough to have them report the Taliban activities.

CBS's distain for America has never been more blatant.

Their filming of the secret Air Command center disclosed that the location was in the Mid-East and pictures and names of military personnel assigned there were broadcast to the world.

Friends and relatives who receive communication from these people and know their location, now can ascertain the location of the command center. What gives?

Why the deliberate attempt to side with the enemy?

Abu Ghraib

Just a thought from an ordinary man. In watching the news unfold about the photos of the treatment of Iraqi prisoners I have my own interpretations of the dilemma.

The dilemma is – our troops don't know who they're fighting. Is it CBS, who chose to make these photos available to the muslin world and the rest of our enemies rather than to take the moral high road and try to quietly fix the perceived problem within the military? Is it the democratic leadership who encourages CBS in the hopes that it will provide political fodder to enhance their candidate, even at the cost of National security and American integrity throughout the world? Or, is it the republican leadership who must now run scared and abandon their course because of political pressure?

What message is now sent to the troops? Regardless of losses, first priority is – 'politically correct' rules. Appease the people who control the press. Regardless of losses! If the enemy is playing by a set of rules which are killing you, so be it, your rules have already been set by someone back home.

It appears that the soldiers accused of these 'uncivilized' acts had been encouraged to fight by a set of rules which are more effective on this type of enemy. In a culture which considers one man seeing another man naked as a sin, and homosexuality as a death sentence, the threat of having pictures such as these circulated throughout the community is probably a greater motivator than physical torture.

Not being there, it is hard to imagine how desperate a soldier would be to obtain information which would keep his comrades from being killed on a daily basis.

What measures should one take to extract this information from a captured enemy who is known to have used women and children as protective cover in battle?

If unconventional interrogation methods save the lives of your fellow soldiers, does that make you a hero of a criminal? What is an American life worth? What is political correctness worth?

I noticed that the general in charge bailed out on this battle because it was a battle she realized she would not win. This battle between political correctness and reality can even separate a general from her army.

In my opinion, when the rules of war are set by the enemy, win by whatever rules are necessary or get out!

If we truly need to be there to keep the battle off American soil . . . WIN. Our soldiers are not there to be martyrs; they are there to be soldiers. With the tools and technology available to them there is no excuse for the loss of ANY Americans. Having served for twenty years I would hate to have given my life for political correctness, a cause I do not believe in.

Thanks for taking the time to read this. I thought it was important.

Thoughts 9/18/04

Feeding Intel to the Enemy

I f you want to know how an 'ordinary man' really feels, here's an
example. I watched the broadcast news reveal how an American
Marine had shot a wounded insurgent only to find out later that the
insurgent did, in fact, pose a threat. That part was not revealed in the
clip. The inaccurate clip was, of course, made public world wide.

I sent the following note to friends that I correspond with by
email:

> I believe that one of the most important questions in
> America today is: WHO gave the incomplete, biased, and
> misleading filmclip of the Marine shooting of the insurgent
> in Iraq to al-Jezeera?
>
> Regardless of the debate over the American public's right
> to know everything, why was this permitted to be obtained
> by al-Jezeera to incite the muslim world against America.
>
> The real debate is – is this TREASON or SEDITION?
> Where's the American public's right to know now? NAME
> NAMES!!!

Marines on Trial

J ust a follow-up thought about our Marines who were recently tried and convicted by ABC News and John Murtha for shooting Iraqi civilians.

As the Marine convoy was blown up and their comrade killed in front of their eyes they were surrounded by enemies who knew of the explosives placed on the road outside their homes. The enemy, though maybe unarmed at that moment, have been walking around this device for some time and waiting for an opportunity to watch Americans die as they passed.

As the enemy waited for the excitement of an American death did they expect this entertainment to be free?

Why does the enemy expect your political correctness and sensitivity training to overcome your fear, confusion, panic, survival instinct, and natural feeling of revenge?

Who among us would have had enough composure to forgive these enemies at the moment of catastrophe and trust that they were not armed, not involved, and had no opportunity to warn you, make a call, identify the bomb, etc.

Once again, I hope these events were reported wrong BUT, if they occurred, let's put ourselves in their shoes.

Thank God these kids volunteer to sacrifice their lives to keep this environment away from American soil.

Given the known conditions of the attack could you, at maybe 19 years of age, overcome all your natural tendencies and walk away and forgive these maggots?

Please forward this with your inputs to help foster empathy for our troops. They deserve a fair trial.

Marines on Trial II

Just a follow-up to keep our troops in our minds and prayers. It appears that the Marines involved in the November incident in Haditha, Iraq are currently in the brig although they have yet to be convicted of a crime. Thank goodness the American press is rooting out the American devils and exposing them to the world.

If your kid at 18 years of age had trouble keeping his room clean how would he react to an enemy attack which killed his best friend. Please don't write off our kids yet.

How many more kids are going to be willing to enlist for a one sided fight where cultural sympathy outweighs survival; where your own news media profits in your demise.

War! What are the answers??? I've got the answers! You pick your choice of any two of the following:

1. Get out. It's not worth it. (Is this realistic? What about the lives that have already been sacrificed?)
2. Get in all the way and win within a month. (Gotta first get rid of the reporters. The press is entitled to their ideology but not a the cost of American lives. If we decide to win we've gotta be prepared to win . . . period.)
3. Reinstall Saddam. Acknowledge that they have a different culture than we do and we will not change five thousand years of breeding. They understand and appreciate only strength, brutality and powerful, uncompromising leadership. We possess none of these at this time.

4. Disregard borders that are already disregarded by our enemies. Strike whatever threatens America, wherever it exists. Apologize later. Do you think this can't be done by the most powerful nation on the planet? We appear to be barely winning in a puss pocket like Iraq because we're fighting on everyone else's terms, by rules that we know are ludicrous.

5. All wars involving America will be fought by the Air Force and Navy. The Army and Marines will *not* be a police force. If it becomes important enough to force us to war it's important enough to win.

6. Decision makers who have the power to commit ground troops must have a relative who is a ground troop.

Meet the Press Hatchet Job 10/5/08

W atching the hatchet job called Meet the Press this morning a question arose in my mind; what is the motivation? They ALL desperately slammed the Republican ticket.

I understand the motivation of the Blacks. I've been there. When JFK was running, every Irish Catholic nun prayed openly in the classrooms for the first Irish Catholic candidate. It was our turn.

Boston has been re-electing the worst of the Kennedy clan for decades. There's no question about his cowardice and dishonesty but there's still blind loyalty. Loyalty I understand. Most Blacks still believe that OJ is innocent of all charges.

What I don't understand though is the motivation of the media for Obama. They avoid addressing his accomplishments because they are educated and they know that he has no accomplishments. They are lying, cheating, and slandering to clear the way for Obama to win. Why?

McCain has never been an enemy of the press so I don't think it's the man. There is a zeal to elect Obama; a distinct terror of losing.

They threw Hillary under the bus for Obama so it's probably not even the party.

They cannot agree with his associations because the distaste of his associates for main stream America is way too obvious. What gives?

Will we ever find out why an election is being bought and paid for? Or who's paying for it.

JACK GORMAN

There is now a hatred for John McCain, a verified hero who can't be hated, by over half of the American public. How the hell did they do this?

Pass this question around enough so that maybe someone in the know will honestly answer it.

Thoughts 9/11/2006

J ust saw Mat Lauer's interview with President Bush. I'm not sure who was worse.

Lauer kept pressing on the techniques being used against terrorists to extract information. His concern being the inhumane methods such as water boarding and other methods which he considers torture. And, he expressed his concern over the use of foreign prisons by the CIA to hold and interrogate captured enemy combatants.

Bush expressed the importance of obtaining information to save American lives and that all was done within the law.

Lauer pressed further about the inhumanity of our methods and Bush repeated his promise to defend America.

The two pressing questions are:

1. How do the American people stop the likes of NBC and their colleagues before their hatred of 'real' America affords more rights to terrorists than our own people enjoy, thereby further crippling our ability to defend ourselves.
2. Will Bush ever use his majority position to rip the heads off the Mat Lauers of the country and make the people who elected him proud?

The small vocal minority of America did not elect Bush. Why does he feel a need to please them rather than pull the stops on the war on terror and do it right? For example: why are we losing troops in the Mid East when we have an Air Force? What real American truly believes that the prevention of collateral damage is more important than the lives of our military? Picture your child on the ground in Afghanistan or Iraq THEN answer the question.

I don't know who I was more disappointed in – Lauer or Bush. America sure needs the leader that we thought Bush was!

Thoughts:
ABC News Crucifying Marines

L etter written to internet buddies.

Just wanted to ask for your help with a situation that I have no other way to handle.

ABC News has decided to cover the story of US Marines who have maybe made the biggest mistake of their lives after being attacked and losing one more of their own in another Iraqi roadside attack. Their handling of their response appears tragic. It's claimed that the Marines killed civilians in response. The situation has been sensationalized to the world including interviews with a 12 year old girl as a witness, all before the official investigation was even completed. By broadcasting this to the world every opportunity has been exhausted to incite more hatred of America for these actions.

I hope the event has not happened as broadcasted. But, if it did, why make it worse? As a 20 year military veteran I feel for our troops even more deeply. You can't have EVERYONE against you ALL THE TIME.

Their days are not like ours. We sacrifice nothing. They sacrifice all. They expect their enemy to try to kill them. Not ABC News!

By taking this moral low road ABC has thrown our troops under a bus for personal gain.

I don't have the opportunity to speak with these decision makers at dinner or at the club. I don't even have the opportunity to whip their butts for the American lives that will be lost because of their reporting tactics. All I can do as an ordinary man is to ask my friends for the help that our troops deserve. Bottom line – ABC News, don't put our troops on trial to incite our enemies, for your personal gain!

Please stop watching ABC. Stop supporting their sponsors. Forward this to EVERYONE you know. If you have ideas on how to make this more effective, tell us so that we can help.

Thoughts: NBC Condemnation of US Marine 11/16/04

The film taken by an imbedded NBC news reporter of the US Marine shooting a wounded enemy in a Falluja mosque has been released to al Jazeera to be shown in entirety. The film shows the name of the Marine even though the US news organizations were told to protect the identity of the Marine because of an ongoing investigation.

Why an imbedded reporter is allowed to participate in live combat is a mystery to me. The next mystery is why questionable film is released to the public resulting in the trial and condemnation of the Marine prior to a proper investigation, and also, WHO gave that film to al Jezeera, *the tool of the enemy*. This film will now be used to incite the enemy to hate the US even further. Will this ever be answered for the American public?

Why is every attempt being made to degrade the US in every way possible? Who (name names) is trying to undermine the success of the US in Iraq? Who wants us to lose face or lose completely in the muslim world? NAME NAMES. Identify the decision makers and let the public decide their fate.